PRAISE FOR *THE ART O*

"Dr. Brennan's new book is a nece.
increase inner awareness, internal calm and expand loving relationships.
He is an individual who has acquired unusual wisdom and we are the
fortunate recipients of his diligent efforts. Every chapter is full of insights
that will provide you and those you love with a path to emotional free-
dom as well as providing a genuine means to reach mature and lasting
love. This is a beautiful book I will be reading and re-reading many
times to fully grasp its growth promoting content."

Dr. Arthur P. Ciaramicoli, Ed.D., Ph.D. Author of *The Power of*
Empathy, Performance Addiction, and The Curse of the Capable.

"There are few books that can literally change your life, and this is
one of them. In The Art of Becoming Oneself, *Dr. James Brennan*
expounds on the wisdom of the ages—from both the West and the
East—in a way that can instantly transform your attitude, your rela-
tionships and your sense of fulfillment."

Kevin Kruse, Author of the *New York Times* **bestseller,** *We*

"This is a truly inspiring and deeply insightful book for those who are
interested in becoming a better leader and more importantly a better
person. In The Art of Becoming Oneself *Dr. Brennan provides a*
guide for a journey that leads to self-knowledge, fulfillment and ulti-
mately greater happiness. I am recommending this book to all my friends
and colleagues."

Jay Wright, Villanova University Men's Basketball Coach

"This is most definitely not another of those insipidly boring self-help
books that has barely one thing to say while saying it too many page-
filling times. Each chapter is concise, to the point and extremely thought
provoking. Just when I thought it had all been written, this book opens
new doors to increasing wisdom while providing innovative mind paths
toward improving self-awareness and inner growth. To say that I was
impressed after reading this work is truly an understatement."

Dr. Sally Headding, Ph.D., Intuitive Counseling Therapist

THE ART OF
BECOMING
ONESELF

To: Ed and Patti Sue
Enjoy the journey.
Jim Brennan

THE ART OF BECOMING ONESELF

A Fresh Interpretation of Our Possibilities

JAMES P. BRENNAN, PH.D.

WORD ASSOCIATION PUBLISHERS
www.wordassociation.com
1.800.827.7903

Printed in the United States of America.

ISBN: 978-1-59571-731-3
Library of Congress Control Number: 2011936485

Designed and published by

Word Association Publishers
205 Fifth Avenue
Tarentum, Pennsylvania 15084

www.wordassociation.com
1.800.827.7903

To Camille with love

Contents

FOREWORD

Suggestions on Using This Work

It is an honor to write the foreword for this book. Having spent many hours immersed in attempting to edit and refine its multiple facets, it has changed me permanently and for the better. New vistas and ways of considering life and its meanings have opened, such that each encounter, each day, is lived differently. Whether this shows in my outward behavior or to those who know me well is not clear. But I know it; it is as if my very DNA has shifted in permanent ways. Hopefully this won't seem like the typical hyperbole of advocacy (though of course it will), perhaps it is best if you as the reader experience this work before you judge my personal experience.

It is from this perspective I offer some thoughts on how to maximize your value as you read. These thoughts are neither exclusive nor exhaustive; they represent my attempt to present a general road map for proceeding. Though as you hopefully will discover, there may be many ways to appreciate this book. It is first suggested that you make your approach with a prepared mind. Many authors writing from an Eastern perspective urge people to place themselves in the right mind-frame before undertaking any activity. In this case, it is recommended you attempt to leave behind expectations and desire, and attempt instead to be unhurried and open. Those who try to "get" this book may find they are frustrated, for it does not lend itself to being readily absorbed or grasped, as perhaps we have become used to finding with the wide array of self-help and self-improvement literature.

As you begin to read, anticipate being confused or contorted at times, while at other times experiencing surprise or a sense of awakening. Sentences may jump out at you; the word combinations will not be unfamiliar, but the meaning of the sentence may seem new or disorienting. Ideally, this will become a pleasant experience, though perhaps at first it will be unnerving.

It is well to not expect to read this work as a novel (i.e. to get to the ending or find the "plot") nor as a guide to living to be read like a cookbook, or X number of steps method to happiness. To do so, one is likely to miss much of what is offered; if tempted to do so, it may be best to return to the paragraph above for thoughts on preparation for reading, in an attempt to re-establish the optimal attitude.

This is a book best kept by a bedside or other favorite reading place. You may prefer to read only one page or chapter at a sitting, choosing to spend as much time as desired considering the points made. It is in short, a deeply contemplative book. The beauty is as much in the journey as the hopeful outcome of self and world improvement.

Engaging in an internal (or shared with others, if possible) dialogue with and about the ideas described within may prove fruitful. That is, writing or speaking quietly or out loud to self and/ or others is likely to enhance your experience. Making notes in the margins or open spaces is highly encouraged. Ideally this book will be shared with others as well -- it is a work not designed or destined for a dusty shelf but for lending to others, at times with no expectation of return.

Though the best effort has been made to arrange the chapters in a sequence that makes experiential sense, it is not required that one read each chapter in the order they appear, and readers may choose certain chapters that appeal to them at any given time. Each chapter can stand by itself as a meditation on the title subject. Of course, to get the fullest exposure to the complexity and gestalt of the ideas contained, it will be well to read and consider all chapters.

Finally, as you turn to the first chapter of this work, a plain description may help prepare you for what to expect. This book is an attempt to synthesize thought/philosophies/ideologies from the breadth of written human history, drawing without preference or prejudice on any and all prior works. It has been extracted and shaped from what has and will continue to exist in the realm of understanding and cultivation of the human experience. There is no intention for it to stand in direct opposition to other dogmas or methods of living, be they spiritual or humanistic; rather it is hoped it will complement and enhance such world views. There may be times however when these views do arouse conflict in the reader's mind, and if this happens, the ensuing struggle will hopefully result in a new synthesis for differential ideas.

To this writer, you are embarking on a deep personal journey; your companion is this compendium of five thousand years of human wisdom. May it impact you with the same profundity I have found.

Edward Lundeen, Ph.D.
Clinical Psychologist

CHAPTER ONE
Covering Our Feet

*"But we must not forget that only a very few people
are artists in life; that the art of life is the most distinguished
and rarest of all the arts."* – **Carl Jung**

This is a book about growth. It is grounded in the premise that human beings exist in a state of pure potential—never as a finished product—and that the skillful use of conscious awareness is essential for actualizing this potential. We need not harbor the belief that the "good life" would be possible if only human nature were made of different and better stuff. Happiness and fulfillment do not come from rare or special qualities, but from our everyday relationships with self, others, and our life circumstances. The resources we need are always present right within us. They comprise our own nature. The good life is about learning to recognize our deeper cognitive, emotional and spiritual resources and using these to evolve toward higher levels of ourselves.

The desire to progress and mature through each life stage, in short, to become more fully human, is the prerogative of every person. It involves learning how to grow, but even more importantly, it is about discovering what to grow *toward*. By virtue of our humanity, we have a legitimate right to set our aspirations high, to pursue what is in us to be, and to enjoy the whole range of our capacities. In fact, gaining a deeper understanding of these capacities is our best motivation for becoming our higher selves.

A renowned Buddhist teacher from the eighth century, named Shantideva, utilized a simple yet profound analogy to illuminate this point. He compared the external conditions of life to the surface of the earth, which contains many rocks, thorns and other hazards capable of injuring us as we move about. Whereas we may wish it were possible to safeguard ourselves from these hazards by covering the entire world with animal hides, he taught that the protection we seek could be achieved merely by the amount of leather it takes to cover our feet. If we know how to keep our feet covered, we can walk anywhere. Likewise, the most direct and efficient way to prepare ourselves to deal with the adverse conditions of the outer world is to cultivate our best inner qualities. In this sense, we learn to cover our feet through greater understanding, mindfulness, patience, humility, kindness, and courage.

Life will continuously present us with favorable opportunities, even in the most unfavorable moments, to change and grow in freedom and wisdom. The more we know and see, the better we will be at choosing our responses and creating our own effects. Our finest asset is the constitution of our own mind, however, the biggest roadblocks are also in our mind. We can have the good life, but we can also miss it. *Growing old is not the same as growing up.* We only need to look around us at the suffering, depression, and greed of modern life to see this regrettable truth.

Our greatest advances as human beings have been for the most part technological, but our greatest problems and challenges remain psychological. These problems are largely issues of consciousness. If we want to significantly increase our chances for happiness, it is best to examine the nature of consciousness itself. In the metaphorical sense, this is how we learn to put the leather around our feet.

This book should be read as a life map. Its purpose is to reveal the larger landscape of human potential by describing the mental qualities most beneficial to those seeking to learn more about themselves. Further, it will encourage readers to elevate the quality of their seeking by bringing attention to the features of human experience that make life worth living. It will not try to persuade the reader to take a specific path, nor aim for an ultimate destination. It will not claim to delineate absolute truth.

We do better to avoid the need to arrive at answers that are fixed and complete, or to bring our search to a final conclusion. Life is best lived as a continuous quest to expand our awareness and use our intelligence to better comprehend the nature of our situation. As each new realization leads to further realizations, we can expect to enjoy a greater degree of daily functioning, wisdom, balance and happiness. Through this progression we also begin to realize how so many of life's problems that present themselves at more basic levels of understanding simply fade away as we learn to see them in a larger context.

The following chapters will examine the aspects of our cognitive, emotional and spiritual repertoire, and describe them in the context of our greater possibilities. The thoughts and ideas expressed within will have very little meaning except to those who are themselves avid seekers of their own true natures.

CHAPTER TWO
Inner Awareness

"Knowing others is intelligence, knowing yourself is true wisdom. Mastering others is strength, mastering yourself is true power." – **Lao-tzu**

Having a feeling is not always the same as "knowing a feeling." What does it mean to be deeply aware of how we are responding to our environment or our situation? How long does it take us to reach the pivotal moment when we realize our emotions are shifting, or to comprehend the impact that each shift might be having? The wise person does not automatically accept the first feelings and thoughts that stream into consciousness, nor does he or she try to assert control over them. He or she simply examines them. The more adept we become at recognizing the emotions and thoughts arising in us, the more freedom we will have to intentionally feed, diffuse, or even re-channel them.

The all-too-common view is that there are few options for managing our current states of mind, which are mostly shaped by our outer circumstances. However, what we ultimately think and how we feel is not forced upon us. By self-examination and inner awareness, we can discover that our states of consciousness are the result of some level of choice. Most of our reactions to stimuli are conditioned responses, or automated behaviors, with accompanying emotional components that are programmed into our habit systems. This automaticity can provide a time-saving advantage when the demands of life are repetitive and predictable, given of course that what is programmed is wise and effective. Fundamental habits can also be helpful for freeing our attention to plan and execute other tasks, or for higher-level guidance, or to create solutions for new problems. But to live exclusively in the world of our habit systems is to forsake many of our higher potentialities. We need a good working balance between our pre-programmed habit systems and our inner awareness.

Because the human brain can observe and reflect upon its own thoughts, emotions, and behaviors, we are capable of continuously refining and re-framing these activities. The more attention we give to this important mental work, the more ability we have to de-automatize and re-direct consciousness. This capacity for conscious oversight, when actively engaged, extends our adaptability by allowing us to override our habit systems and challenge our own assumptions and convictions whenever we want. When this level of inner awareness is highly active, we can participate in a more impartial and intelligent dialogue with ourselves.

Wisdom begins in this realm of impartiality, where our power to choose also begins. In effect, we are creating more spacious areas of consciousness where we are much less susceptible to feeling psychologically cornered or out of positive options. From here it is possible to find or regain our balance in any situation. Inner awareness equates to inner freedom, and inner freedom is possible at any moment—as long as we remember that it is. This is not a trick of the mind, but rather an agility of mind that allows us to recognize and adjust our perspective more quickly, and to choose our responses deliberately and intelligently.

The more we learn to process reality in this way—adjusting our thoughts, and feelings, and behaviors as we wish—the more we are in charge of constructing our lives and plotting our relationship with our world. Free will can only operate in conjunction with inner awareness. They are a tandem operation and the power of the former will naturally be proportional to the range of the latter. Free actions are never totally free but will always occur within a context of limitations. However, free will and self-determination seem to expand as we rise to higher levels of self-reflection.

If we simply watch the flow of our own mental activity as if we were watching the weather, we realize that we don't need to become attached to every thought or emotion that arises. We can choose to let them drift in and out of conscious attention like clouds passing across the sky. By shifting our self-identification from what is being observed to that of the impartial observer, we essentially loosen the grip the thinking mind has on us. We can maintain the freedom to say: "these thoughts and feelings I am watching are not really mine unless I decide to become more involved in them," or "I am **not** them, I am merely observing them." Thoughts or feelings that, in our judgment, are wise to avoid do not need to be repressed or over-controlled. If we do not feed them and make them stronger, they will get weaker and eventually die. Opinions and feelings are not in themselves dangerous to us if we know how to hold them loosely and own them provisionally.

Through the practice of inner awareness, we also begin to discover how it is possible to avoid clashing with negativity. We can transcend the negative, more limited perspective by simply choosing the broader, more positive position. Well-being requires the ability to re-contextualize our situation, and expand our perspective to a bigger picture where negative emotions cannot linger. As we learn to bring greater amounts of pertinent information into the light—in terms of our external and internal circumstances—we use inner awareness to increase conscious awareness, which becomes the means through which we can significantly shape and elevate our lives. The abilities of free will, free choice, circumspection, and sound judgment all derive from this process.

As human beings we tend to operate as if reality comes primarily from external happenings but the source of all experience is a sensing from within. Inner awareness, extended to its maximum powers, leads to the realization that there is no natural dichotomy between inner and outer because they are the same. Each of us is an inseparable part of the totality, an expression of the whole. However, we must rely on our own bodies and minds as the primary instruments of our perceptions and experiences. There is no possibility of knowing anything at all other than through subjectivity. Happiness is subjectively produced and so is meaning. Even negative experiences can be given positive meaning. Through the proper use of awareness we can choose to be in a positive or negative state. This choice can be purely up to each individual. Each moment of awareness is a moment of choice.

The capacity to create a life that overflows with happiness and love is our birthright, and it is also our responsibility. No one else can do it for us. We are the authors and the authorizers of this life we are experiencing. Potentially, we have the power to be masters of our fate, and in the long run, the character of our lives is determined by how we cultivate and utilize this power. The search for the source of all things and the search for the source of ourselves are the same. It is progressively inward. When we have the ability to come back to ourselves again and again, we find that there are endless ways of doing what we want to do and of being the people we want to be. As Socrates said, "Know thyself."

CHAPTER THREE

A Deep Sense of Purpose

*"Do not be too moral. You may cheat yourself out of
much life. Aim above morality. Be not simply good, be good
for something."* – **Henry David Thoreau**

If the most important thing about what appens to us is shaped
by how we subjectively experience it, how then do we intentionally elevate our subjective experience to its highest levels? It
is natural to feel a more intense intrinsic motivation and desire
when we are engaged in challenges that come from our values,
hopes, affections and visions. Our deeper purposes are contained
in the things that seem to really grab our attention and raise our
energy level. What is my gift? What are my aspirations? What do
I care about? What is my truth? These are the kinds of questions
that we ought to be asking ourselves daily, and the best answers
cannot be handed down to us by others. No one else can rightly

name them or assign them. As the old adage goes, "The acorn knows what the tree should be."

The life path that follows our deeper sense of purpose is one that continuously coaxes us along our growth continuum toward each succeeding level of our inherent abilities. It is often more difficult than other life paths, but also far more inspiring because it follows what is already encoded in our unique human design. Becoming ourselves requires a lot of work, but feels intrinsically rewarding because it is *our* work. On the other hand, putting our effort into becoming someone we are not is perhaps the most difficult work of all—and it only undermines our happiness.

One's deeper sense of purpose might be thought of as a form of self knowledge that operates below the level of conscious awareness, and shapes our development through the kinds of issues that we take more seriously, such as our religious or philosophical beliefs. These become the bases of self-governing concepts like truth, justice, love, compassion, and so forth that direct us from the inside out, rather than from the outside in. They exert a strong influence over the way we think, behave, and generally construct our lives. They can function like an internal navigation system, using our own personal compass points—in the form of our needs and potentials—to guide us through all kinds of outer conditions.

To discover these deeper purposes, we must learn to be more aware of the intuitive signals they send, and to trust ourselves enough to act on them. Intuition is a higher form of intelligence than logical reasoning; however, it is not as easily accessible because its messages are often nuanced and subtle. In our modern culture, where the abilities for memory, computation, and logical problem-solving are the marks of intelligence, we typically are not taught to cultivate our intuitive powers, and we may assign lesser value to them. Nonetheless, intuitive information is continuously being transmitted.

We all know what it is to experience certain moments or situations in which we feel most like ourselves, when we have a strong sense that we are in our element. If we learn to give higher importance to these moments and to pay close attention to what our thoughts and feelings are conveying, we will have an opportunity to perceive important clues about our innate blueprint. These clues will come by way of our inner longings, our sense of excitement, our intrinsic gratification, and sometimes through a heightened awareness of our own possibilities. As we become more sensitized to these signals, we will find ourselves gravitating more toward certain challenges, if for no other reason than our involvement in the work itself feels more motivating.

When we are fortunate enough to be immersed in activities that make us feel like the right person at the right time doing the right things for the right reasons, what we are experiencing is the unified participation of the *whole person*, mind, body, and spirit. Precisely through such synergistic experiences we discover our deeper purposes; however, the realization is based more on feelings than logical comprehension. It is a knowing that resonates more through our heart than our reasoning mind, which is probably why we are so prone to discount its validity.

As we increase our awareness of our deeper sense of purpose, we begin to see how virtually everything that comes into our lives can teach us something we would do well to know. It is as if we are partaking in a progressive series of lessons that keep arriving just when we are most ready to learn them. If we put more trust in our inner form, we will become better at the art of continuously re-creating and refining our outward approach to life, while at the same time strengthening our core of personal consistency. Our decisions and actions will be guided by a fluid, adaptive intelligence rather than a rigid set of rules handed down to us by someone else. If we make an effort to be the best "me" in each situation, and try to give our highest quality response to the needs of that particular moment, our personal brand of quality will be evident, and it will provide a basis of stability to a life that is rapidly evolving.

We do not exist accidentally; we are here meaningfully. Perhaps this concept is best illustrated by the effect that a deeper sense of purpose has for all human beings. That is, it links the self with something beyond the self, something greater. Psychological well-being, wherever it exists, must be sustained by a balanced desire to be a contributing member of the world at large while simultaneously pursuing personal fulfillment. It is natural to want to believe that life in its total range has worth and significance and that we are somehow playing an active role in that significance. This is why the development of our higher nature will always require a larger context or cause within which we can effectively carry out our personal journeys. In fact, whenever we are feeling emotionally out of balance, it is usually a sign that we are overcommitted to the self (in the limited sense of the term) and under committed to the greater good.

The synergies produced between our selves and our relations with life arise from the emotional rather than the material world. Emotional power will always have its roots in personal meaning and the quality of the meaning we make will be determined by the significance we place on life itself. Too many people wake up each day to furiously pursue the things they mistakenly believe will make them happy, not realizing that they already have what is needed. They are like the confused cowboy who saddles up and rides out to look for his horse. Happiness is not something out there. It does not come from events or circumstances, but instead from the meaning we derive from them. The same is true for unhappiness. A life without deeper meaning will sooner or later bring misery and emptiness.

CHAPTER FOUR
Engaging the Heart

"The dream of man's heart, however much he may distrust and resent it, is that life may complete itself in a significant pattern. Some incomprehensible way. Before death. Not irrationally but incomprehensibly fulfilled." – **Saul Bellow**

The heart is a great source of positive emotional energy because it is the epicenter of human inspiration. This is also where things we care about most are generated and stored. The heart is where we foster values and purposes bigger than our individual selves and deeper than our everyday lives. It is the central rhythmic organ of the body and influences the regulation of both physiological and emotional processes during our everyday functioning. It could be said that our body's various energy fields vibrate around the heart just as the planets orbit around the sun.

The heart transmits a deeper knowledge that is not intellectual in form. In contrast to the reasoning mind, it does not seek quantifiable understanding or rely on rational analysis. Instead, it operates through the emotions to influence the quality of our experiences. The heart "feels" what it knows and its wisdom springs from a more primordial source than that of the brain. The synergy that is produced between the heart and mind arises from the emotional, not the material world. The Buddhists believe the heart to be the source of all the positive emotions, and even in our own culture there are many common expressions that reference the heart as an emotional center. We say that we feel love "in our hearts." Our sincerity "comes from the heart." If we are working toward a goal with great dedication, we say that we are "putting our hearts into it." When we are being courageous, we are showing "a lot of heart."

From the standpoint of consciousness, the heart creates a realm of inner sensing, a private presence, a connection to the universe that is available only to its owner. The heart is far more than a pump; it is also an organ of great intelligence, and highly sensitive to our emotions. Even the slightest emotional shifts are registered more powerfully in the heart than in the brain, and the heart informs the rest of the nervous system. This is how life conveys its invisible information directly to us. If we are receptive to these messages, they can teach us, deepen us, and make us grow. We might reject our heart signals, disregard them, or even forget about them, but the heart will still insistently communicate what it feels. It does not forget us. Whether we like it or not, the heart affects our reasoning, our choices, our emotions, and our perceptions. As Martin Buber wrote, "We may ignore our inner nature, we may silence it, but we can never uproot it."

Reality is multi-dimensional. It has many forms and, consequently, it is perceived and expressed in many different ways. The realm of reasoning seeks a quantifiable understanding of life through intellectual analysis, while the realm of feeling seeks inspiration through the use of emotions. In the worlds of education, business, and everyday commerce, the reasoning mind enjoys a much greater status. As a matter of convention, our culture has made the reasoning mind the master and the heart merely a servant. Unfortunately, we have this arrangement backwards. Just as the body is the instrument of the mind, the mind is the instrument of the heart.

The logical mind and the heart speak different languages that are not easily translatable to each other. The logical mind can acquire knowledge but cannot animate and vitalize what it knows. It cannot generate positive meaning from the experiences of joy, pain, fear, or sadness. Life is much more complicated than the logical mind can comprehend. In fact, one of the biggest impediments to higher levels of understanding is the logical mind's interference with the processes of deeper consciousness, which operate more intimately with the interdependencies of life.

Most of us have experienced times when we have allowed ourselves to be guided by our emotionally toned thoughts, putting our trust in what "feels right" without knowing all the details. And we may even have sensed, in a generalized way that life was coaxing us in the right direction just as migrating birds instinctively sense when it is time to fly north or south. This level of feeling is indicative of the inner voice of the heart, and its role is to help us uncover and direct our unique talents.

The finest example of this synchronicity we can ever know in life is love. Love is surely a state that cannot be known logically. The reasoning mind can observe love from a distance and can even try to describe it, but only the heart can feel love's energy. Sometimes this energy can be translated through music, art, poetry or some other form of aesthetic expression, but if we are not experiencing love through our hearts, we are not experiencing it at all.

True understanding of life happens through the heart, because the heart will ultimately determine the meaning and quality of our experiences. The reasoning mind can never create deep happiness, because happiness is an emotional state that cannot be quantified. The moment we try to analyze happiness, we begin to inhibit our pure experience of it. Although logical analysis can assist us in making a living, only the heart can guide us in making a meaningful life. Only by living through the heart can we discover the value of our own existence. This is why, in terms of the human machinery, the reasoning mind was designed to be the servant, while the heart was designed to be the master.

CHAPTER FIVE

Commitment

*"Concerning all acts of initiative (and creation),
there is one elementary truth which the ignorance of kills countless ideas and splendid plans: that the moment one definitely
commits oneself, then Providence moves too. All sorts
of things occur to help one that would never otherwise
have occurred."* — **Johann Wolfgang von Goethe**

Commitment holds a magical and mysterious emotional power, which might be why we are often so afraid of it. Whenever life presents us with an opportunity to risk and struggle our way to the next level of our personal maturation, the fear of failure can arise and undermine our self confidence and our positive focus. In this state of mind, our predominant outlook is more likely to be one of caution, and our thought processes will urge us to hold back for a myriad of logical reasons. We begin to think that now is not the very best time to take such a big step, or that we might not be the right person to take it. After all, who is ever perfectly prepared for any important and difficult venture?

Whenever we are facing a precarious and demanding challenge, the common reaction is to refrain from committing fully until we feel at least reasonably assured that we will succeed. Ironically, this is the very perspective that undermines the greatest advantage commitment brings; our most difficult pursuits are more likely to succeed only *after* we have fully committed to them. By contrast, each time we choose to take an unnecessary precaution against the potential of failure, we have already allowed ourselves to become the victims of our fear of failure. Commitment is the antidote to this kind of fear, because it is the mind's way of pre-accepting responsibility for the consequences of not succeeding. This pre-acceptance actually allows us to be less troubled by the threat of failure and instead, to be more focused on the pursuit of success.

Each of us possesses two opposing sets of motivational instincts: 1) the conservative instincts for self-preservation, playing it safe and saving energy, and 2) the growth and development instincts of exploring, creating, enjoying novelty and risk. The first set of instincts requires little encouragement or support from the outside to motivate behavior. This makes sense because it is usually much easier to be passive towards life, to hold back and play it safe. The second set of instincts, however, is more focused on growth than safety, and this motivational system, which promotes striving and risk taking, will atrophy if not intentionally cultivated. We do this by allowing ourselves to take on difficult challenges and to be exposed to a certain amount of adversity. It simply is not possible to grow stronger and happier by running away from life's challenges.

When we are facing our challenges, it is important to remember that the advantage goes to those who are willing to start, not perfectly prepared, yet willing to fully commit themselves to each step along the way. As the novelist Albert Camus wrote, "Sometimes life calls on us to make a 100 percent commitment to something about which we are only 51 percent sure." Each time we give our full commitment to something, there is an emotional shift and positive motivation is unleashed in the direction of our goals.

Commitment opens us up to the empowering energy of willingness and keeps us from being divided against ourselves. By committing, we are announcing to ourselves and those around us that we are saying no to fear and yes to self-belief, and that we are willing to pay the price required to bring our goals into reality.

There is something intrinsically gratifying about setting goals in desired directions and then committing ourselves to the pursuit of them. It is as if the human energy system calls to us, "Give me something to fully commit to so that I can feel the thrill of elevating myself."

CHAPTER SIX
Enthusiasm

*"Life's blows cannot break a person whose spirit is warmed at
the fire of enthusiasm."* – **Norman Vincent Peale**

Enthusiasm has been called the "panacea of human nature"
because it is perhaps the most available remedy for all forms of
emotional negativity. Both the heart and mind seek enthusiasm.
It is an emotion that quickly rearranges the energy within
us and allows our natural strengths to become fully engaged in
whatever we are doing. Under the influence of a healthy, realistic enthusiasm, we are more in tune with our best thinking
and problem solving abilities. We tend to be less reactive and
defensive, more confident and highly motivated. We communicate more effectively, are more open to collaboration, and make
wiser decisions.

Each mood or attitude introduces its own reality to our consciousness. For the most part, we don't see things as they are; we see them as **we** are. Our perspective is a reflection of our internal state. If we want to be fully alive, we must not only minimize the stressors in life but also learn to actively cultivate the joyful, loving, fulfilling experiences that stimulate personal growth and well being. This is especially important when we experience life as not going well. Too often, we allow ourselves to fall into the state of discouragement because someone has done us wrong or we have made a mistake and we think we deserve to feel badly about it.

At times like this, discouragement may seem like the natural and appropriate response but we should also be aware that it is definitely the weaker response. The adversity itself, whatever it is, will have brought its own penalties. That is bad enough. But do we even consider the penalty we are imposing on ourselves when we choose discouragement over enthusiasm? Do we realize how difficult it is to make a bad situation better when we allow ourselves to come under the influence of negative emotions? If we make a mistake, it is wise to hate the mistake but at the same time love the struggle to make things better. In that way, realities are not denied but instead reframed to make us smarter, tougher, and even more enthusiastic. We are not disregarding the harsher aspects of what has happened, we are merely disregarding the discouragement that often comes with negative circumstances.

Enthusiasm is not simply a way to cope with life's pressures. It takes us beyond coping, which implies that we are merely surviving or enduring, and allows us to express our talents when we need them most. If we are simply coping, we are holding back from committing our best energy, and life will eventually wear us down. Most of the challenges and tasks we face each day are not inherently pleasant or unpleasant. Virtually any activity can be made into drudgery, and most, if not all, activities can be enjoyable if we approach them with an enthusiastic attitude. To the enthusiastic mind, all days, all events, all circumstances bring opportunities.

Enthusiasm is readily available to us because it is an emotion that multiplies whenever it is shared. Anytime we feel the need for more enthusiasm in ourselves, we should look for opportunities to bring it to life in someone else. The more we focus on generating this energy and giving it to others, the more it will come alive in us. If we know that something gives us joy, peace, or happiness, we should not hold back from allowing those around us to participate in our enjoyment, because the very sharing of positive things brings fulfillment.

There is a strong interrelationship between our attitude, thoughts, physiology, and behavior. Cultivating enthusiasm is the easiest and most effective way to create positive changes in all aspects of this total process. There is no need to go somewhere else to find the mental requirements for happiness and well being. We only need to discover our innate ability to deliberately generate this high quality emotional state in our own minds. Enthusiasm is like a strong current of electricity available to anyone who learns how to flick the switch. If we can bring the power of enthusiasm to our most important creative activities, there will be increased energy, intensity, and intelligence behind whatever we are doing. What could be more empowering than the ability to say, "I know how to be happy, therefore I know that I will be happy."

CHAPTER SEVEN
Authenticity
(Remembering Who We Are)

*"There is, at the surface, infinite variety of things:
[but] at the center there is simplicity of cause. How many
are the acts of one man in which we recognize the
same character!"*– **Ralph Waldo Emerson**

When we face difficult life choices, we reduce large amounts
of pressure almost immediately by simply remembering who we
are. Each of us possesses an inner power that lies not so much
in the roles we play, or the circumstances we face, but rather in
our ability to be essentially the same person in every situation.
If we develop a deep trust in our authenticity, not simply blind
trust, but trust based on experience, courage and self-knowledge,
we can make the complicated look simple, the difficult look
easy. Some may believe that being the same person in every
situation requires us to be firm and inflexible. However, when

we observe the people we admire most, we see that what they hold in common is the unusual extent to which they allow their uniqueness to flow freely. They seem to know what is best, what they stand for, and what they deeply need.

The greatest contribution we can make to others is to learn to be the guides of our own lives. We are unique. Our uniqueness does not need to be invented; it is already within us. Our job is to discover and expose this uniqueness to the circumstances around us. We grow faster when we take our own path wherever it leads. Each day the challenges of life unfold and so do we as we work, learn, and grow through them. As long as we remember to be our "best selves" and to respond to each situation according to our own insight, intuition, and intelligence, whatever eventuates will surely suit us. No doubt, there will be times when we are severely criticized for our choices, but such criticism can sound like praise to our ears if we are satisfied in knowing we acted from our own wisdom and best intentions, not from imitation or someone else's manipulation. Risking all to be ourselves, to decide for ourselves, to stand on our own two feet, is the greatest courage. This is powerful. This is true maturity.

We influence others more by what we are than what we say, or do, or own; therefore, we should always begin and end with who and what we are. This is the only way to find our own truth, because all truth is ultimately subjective. Everything we experience and learn, and all the wisdom and meaning that comes from these experiences is, therefore, also subjective. There is no escaping the fact that we are the primary instruments of our perceptions as well as our interpretations of those perceptions.

The most important things we can learn and know can only be found in our experience. That is why it is appropriate to grant ourselves final authority but also ultimate responsibility.

When we are mindful and we remember who we are, all that we experience can be used to take ourselves forward. Yet when we forego mindfulness, even our opportunities can look like obstacles. The outer circumstances themselves are not nearly as important as the quality of our inner awareness. When we respond to whatever is happening with a mind guided by kindness, gratitude, courage, and compassion, we feel a greater energy rising. Our abilities become focused and concentrated. We have mastery of our own mind. Nothing can dominate us, at least not for very long. Life may send us all the wrong circumstances, but it does not matter because we know how to use whatever happens to become stronger inside; this is the strength that counts most. Everything we do then becomes a measured and purposeful response, not a reaction that feels forced upon us by someone else.

There is an ancient Buddhist metaphor involving a burning torch and a river. If someone throws a burning torch into a river, it will burn until the moment it hits the water, then the fire will go out because the river's intrinsic nature is not to burn. When we remember how to be authentic, we will not be compelled to overreact in the face of someone else's negativity. We will not be tricked into playing a role that someone else may want to assign to us. We will not feel the need to *re-act* at all, but instead simply to act, to respond according to our own higher nature. The more we understand ourselves, our best selves, the more we become *response-able*. In this state of mind, we can be like a river, serene and powerful but not flammable. The internal dialogue of a well-balanced person in the middle of strife might sound like this:

"I refuse to accept your hate, your anger, your jealousy, your panic. If you choose to use these emotions against me, I will be little disturbed by them. They will have no power over me. Then what will you do if you cannot wound me? You will be left feeling impotent and I can only hope that for your sake you will one day become tired of wounding yourself."

CHAPTER EIGHT

Self Deception
(Are We Who We Think We Are?)

"It ain't the things we don't know that gets us into trouble, but the things we're sure we know that ain't really so." – **Will Rogers**

There are people who refuse to look at how they can grow. They think they're fine and do not need to change. There are others who greatly underestimate themselves or are held back by the inhibitions of low self-esteem. Both are problems of self-deception, and whenever self-deception distorts or corrupts self-knowledge, it works directly against our aspirations of becoming our best selves. The process of human growth begins within us and works outward as the self engages the outer world. Thus self-deception is among the most self-limiting inclinations we can ever allow ourselves to sustain. It makes us feel right when we are wrong, encourages us to

speak when we do better to listen, and emboldens us to take
win/lose stances when we might search for peaceful solutions
through deeper understanding. And most important, we are all
susceptible to self-deceptive practices.

Perceiving ourselves and our conditions realistically is vital. We
cannot adapt effectively to what we cannot see clearly, or to that
which we should know but are not aware of at all. We make life
harder on ourselves and others whenever we take a misinformed
approach to our circumstances. The one person we should never
lie to is ourselves, but though we may know this we are still
quite vulnerable to self-deception because we become expert at
doing it in ways we cannot easily detect. Even when we operate
with the most honest intentions, we are bound up in an inherent conflict of interest. Individual consciousness presents us with
a sense of ourselves out of all proportion to the sense we have
about others.

The belief that "I am in here" and the world is "out there" leads
us to an over attachment to "me," "myself," and "I" that inevitably sets us up for many self-limiting thoughts and behaviors.
This self-centered way of experiencing the world is itself a great
deception and we must recognize and account for it if we are
to avoid its pitfalls. We do well to consider that whatever feels
hurtful to this narcissistic perspective is typically good for the
pursuit of higher truth.

We are each individual beings; at the same time we are interpersonal beings; it is far easier to be sensitive to the first part then
to the second. This creates a disadvantage that is compounded

when we believe that only we know what we need to do to change and grow. As such, the ability to take feedback well is the best way to counteract self-deception and to improve ourselves, while also making our relationships with others stronger. There is a significant difference between the inner voice of self-confidence that says, "I know myself and I don't need feedback from others" and that which says, "I am confident because I can actively listen and process negative feedback about myself."

In the long run, self-deception leads to misery and strife, for ourselves, others, or both. If we fail to look at ourselves, we have no choice but to blame our problems on others. When we are upset it is easier to see others' faults than to see our own. It is also easier to believe others are the primary cause of our unhappiness, and if we could only change them or their behavior we would be happy. It is far more effective to ask, "What is my role in contributing to these reactions in others and in me?" Happiness that is based on deeper understanding is more realistic and enduring. Every time we increase self-understanding we are reducing the limiting effects of self-deception.

There are times when we find ourselves deeply offended by others' negative remarks about us. But when such remarks sting or really hit a nerve, it may be because some part of us already knows they are true. If we were not trying to hide the truth from ourselves and others, we could easily accept what has been said as old news that we have already faced and accepted. On the other hand, if we know with confidence that no part of the remark is true, we should be able to dismiss it as false and move on without much emotional upheaval.

Pain and agitation can take us forward in life, or take us sideways. Whenever we are ready to blame other people for our agitation, we do well to ask ourselves if our responses are moving us in the direction we truly wish to go. If we can condition our minds to bear the discomfort of self-scrutiny or the scrutinies coming from others a little longer than we usually do, we increase our opportunity to learn something valuable. Going beyond our frequent immediate impulse to take a self-defensive position eliminates the need for self or other condemnation. Rather, we find the chance for greater understanding. Truly, we offer ourselves finer self-protection when rather than loathe our mistakes, we loathe the barriers of pretension we erect to prevent us from learning all that we can from those mistakes, or to keep us from repeating these same mistakes over and over.

If we can be at least mildly self-critical we are less prone to resent the criticisms of others, even when delivered with malice. This approach may make us feel more vulnerable but we are actually more adaptive, flexible, resilient, and in the long run self-protective, when we are open to feedback rather than when we fear it. The ability to sift non-defensively through the criticisms from others, to separate what is valid from what is invalid with the intention of learning from both, serves as an excellent definition of wisdom.

Our subjective version of the *truth* is meant to be adaptive in the direction of our personal concerns. If we are full of insecurities, our truths will be more protective. If we are in growth mode, our truths will reveal many opportunities. Rather than taking the view that growth is mostly about eradicating the negatives, we can focus instead on building upon our strengths and culti-vating the positives. We need not hate our faults, but rather we can love our strengths and our potential to develop them further. Let our primary orientation toward becoming ourselves be a commitment to the good, not the avoidance of discomfort. We need not defeat the negative but only transcend it by choosing the positive. With this attitude, our efforts will not be fear-based but motivated by humility, compassion, and gratitude.

Our security is found not in the ability to control our circum-stances, or in having things a certain way (which makes it neces-sary to resist others who will want to see it, have it, do it *their* way), but in our ability to adapt, watch, learn, and tolerate the discomfort that often comes with honest self analysis. If we need to take a hard stand, let it be against giving in to the temptation to default to a simplistic view of things that are really quite com-plicated and multi-layered.

Each moment of life is something new and original in Nature and we should be paying attention to the signals that suggest how we should keep changing too. Imagine living each day with an attitude of awareness, fearlessness, and curiosity. The more we learn to bear the discomfort of opposing self-deception, the more adaptable we will become and the less discomfort we will actually need to endure. We will enjoy more freedom and choic-es while bearing fewer burdens. We will come to learn that the happiness we experience from reducing our insecurities is much greater than the happiness we experience from indulging them.

Understanding ourselves, our flaws, and our susceptibility to errors in judgment does not put us in greater danger. Rather, it allows us to have a looser, more flexible hold on our reality, beliefs, decisions, and actions. It leaves us open to continuous self-evaluation and feedback from others. There is great freedom from admitting that we do not always "know ourselves." It is better to continue learning about ourselves as we go, just as we learn about life as we go. Life is not solid and fixed, but a fluid, interdependent process. So are we. So is our intelligence.

CHAPTER NINE
Perseverance

"All endeavors call for the ability to tramp the last mile, shape the last plan, endure the last hour's toil. The fight to the finish spirit is the one...characteristic we must possess if we are to face the future as finishers." – **Henry David Thoreau**

Perseverance is our psychological muscle. It is an inner discipline, an inner strength that, once developed, gives us the ability to make ourselves do what we don't necessarily want to do, or what is not easy, in order to achieve what we want to achieve. Building this muscle is a demanding task and no one else can do it for us. We are responsible for it, though this is an irritable supposition for many people to accept.

Whenever the road becomes particularly hard, some find it easier to conclude that the whole effort is not worth the trouble. They invest themselves instead in building rational excuses for giving up. Consequently, they learn to live with more excuses and less growth. When they fail, they'd rather believe it is not their fault, that somebody else is holding them back. But others cannot really hold us back, not if we are ready and determined to move ourselves forward by one set of means or another. Experience reveals to us a consistent, albeit harsh, rule of life: the farther extents of wisdom, happiness, and fulfillment shall always remain beyond the reach of those who quit too easily.

It does not require much effort to maintain a solid faith in ourselves when things are going well, or when success seems imminent. What is far more valuable, however, is the ability to keep struggling when the positive outcome is not in sight, when success is not guaranteed. Sometimes we are most tempted to give up just when we are about to succeed, because we often cannot see success until it is well into its onset. The thresholds for breaking *down* versus breaking *through* are seldom far apart. That is why we should develop the habit of asking ourselves during pivotal moments, "Do I make the choice to give up or grow up?" If our answer is to grow up, then our next question becomes, "How do I become bigger than the problem?" Utilizing this kind of approach, we are more likely to remember that the problem is never more important than our response to it.

So many success stories are about someone's resilience in the face of hardship. Even extreme adversity can help us to discover our emotional power if we operate from the premise that the elements necessary for success are always contained in the forces of defeat. In the words of the ancient philosopher Seneca, "Fire is the test of gold, and adversity the test of strong men."

Succeeding through difficult times has less to do with the specific strategies we employ and more to do with our inner conviction and resolve to face our challenges, deal with them fully, and move ahead. When we have a highly developed sense of our own durability and resiliency, we can experience pain and even the beginning stages of breakdown without suffering from self-defeating thoughts.

Hard times are the crucible of character because our personal values mean little until they are tested. Developing the emotional and intellectual toughness needed to deal effectively with adversity is a struggle; it is a strenuous, uphill climb, but the only way we can reach our own peaks. There are no helicopter rides to the top of this mountain. In fact, the further we go in life, the more we come to realize that the things we get for free are seldom useful to our growth. There is far greater joy in rewards that are hard earned. Until we embrace this reality, we cannot begin to expand our powers of creativity, courage, fortitude, persistence, and resilience.

People who don't give up easily are usually those who give themselves positive and meaningful goals. They are often at their very best when circumstances are the worst because they are not easily swayed off course by negativity. They know how to use adversity to create a sense of urgency in themselves, a sort of "on" switch signaling that it is now up to them to do something. They actually like having their backs to the wall because they experience the elevation of their strengths and talents. Their natural response to a setback is, "There must be a way to turn things around and to make this setback useful, and I'll do whatever it takes to find it!" Fortified by this kind of perspective, they find it mentally and emotionally easier to embrace the difficulties for the sake of the opportunities.

Every test that we pass by going deeper into ourselves and finding added strength and self-confidence makes us more capable of leading our own lives with courage and intelligence. Everything that happens to us that makes us want to give up, we can use as a means for waking up to greater insights. A challenge that sets us back one day will probably be repeated again in one form or another, but if we are able to persevere, we will not be derailed again by the same situation. We will have learned something. A deeper understanding will be there.

Perseverance is the internal guarantor that affords us the necessary time and opportunity for all of our other winning capacities to grow to fruition. Those who strive for perseverance enjoy a greater freedom to create their own lives than those who are emotionally frail. And the more we actively create our own lives, the more our freedom increases.

CHAPTER TEN

Courage

"You cannot be truthful if you are not courageous
You cannot be loving if you are not courageous
You cannot be trusting if you are not courageous
You cannot inquire into reality if you are not courageous
Hence courage comes first and everything else follows."
– Osho

Even though we possess a strong intrinsic motivational drive to grow and develop, there is another equally significant part of our emotional make-up whose primary function is to keep us safe and secure. Each new level of progress in life seems to bring us to a physiological or psychological threshold where we must dissolve fear and doubt while increasing courage and self-confidence. There is an internal sense of agitation or even dread whenever we are about to make a big breakthrough, or when we are required to go further than we've ever gone before, where the next stage is unknown. These are the pivotal moments that often make us feel most vulnerable. It is as if life is asking us to decide whether we trust more in our fear, or in our courage.

Courage is not the absence of fear. In fact, the benefits of courage can only be discovered and developed when we are fully aware of our fear. Courage is what initially gives us the ability to *do it afraid*, even if we're not yet prepared to do it well. Once we give ourselves permission to be afraid, and further, to take the next step forward despite our fear, we will expand and improve our proficiency simply through the effort. As we learn to do a thing better, fear subsides and self-confidence grows. Courage bolsters all of our other attributes and talents at their tipping point. The role of courage is to help us learn to tip ourselves forward.

When fear is the dominant factor in how we run our lives, things usually turn out poorly. Each time we choose fear, we reinforce our sense of insecurity. If fear becomes a deep-rooted pattern, our tendencies toward safety and security will grow disproportionately and life will be an endless stream of worrisome events that feed our anxiety and erode our confidence. We will become little more than risk managers. Eventually, we will confuse the feeling of being afraid to do something with the belief that we cannot or should not do it.

Through courage, we can prevent ourselves from investing so much energy into fear. There is an important difference between having fear and being under its spell. When we lean on courage we are investing our energy in self-trust. We may have fear but it does not have us. Courage provides an alternative. It gives us the psychological space to operate with freedom, and freedom from fear allows us to put more of our focus and effort into being happy and effective.

There are times in life when being joyful requires the highest test of courage. Often we cannot permit ourselves to enjoy the blessings of today because we are not over some past hurt or because we know that tomorrow will bring even more hurt. Of course it will; the elements of hurt and joy are always near. They come with life's continuously changing circumstances. Yet it is never wise to huddle in bitterness or misery when the hardships arrive. Good times should be cherished precisely because they do *not* last, and tough times, even tragic times, will eventually run their course also. Our job is to learn from hard times when they come, and to see through and beyond them.

To be miserable over an extended period of time is usually a very cowardly response. When we are miserable we are experiencing the cowardly side of ourselves. Nothing is needed to react this way. Life has sufficient challenges and sorrows to make any of us miserable. Everybody is capable of languishing in self-pity, but to be joyful in a life that brings pain can be a daunting task; often, great courage is needed. Some find it easier to conclude that the whole effort is not worth the trouble, so they invest instead in misery and live for sympathy rather than happiness. Sympathy is an interpersonal medicine with great healing qualities, but only in the short term. If we allow ourselves to rely on it too much, it will weaken our spirit, erode our courage, and become a substitute for self-responsibility.

Extinguishing worry requires the acceptance of the things we fear. This is how we become free from the fear itself; the fear of failing, of loneliness, of destitution, of sickness, and of dying. We cannot become familiar with our own courage unless we give ourselves permission to face our fears. Often, what we call bravery is merely the repression or the denial of fear. The true power of courage is felt when we realize that fear is a natural part of life. We should not create strategies to resist it or hide it. It is seldom wise to run away from our troubles. In fact, whenever the mind feels troubled, it is usually helpful to adopt the perspective that we are only agitated by the life lessons we are ready to learn next.

Although anger can produce short-term courage, it seldom results in the right brand of courage. When we allow our tempers to go unchecked, we become like cans of gasoline waiting for a match to fall in. This emotional state leaves us very vulnerable because we become fair game for anyone who wants to ignite us. Anger is typically a sign of fear and insecurity. It can resemble courage but it is false courage. When we refuse another's invitation to lose our temper we are simulating the finely measured reactions of a highly skilled matador who can calmly but alertly watch the angry bull and know just when to take a small side step and let him go charging by. When we learn not to give into fear, we will no longer feel the need to create fear in anyone else—just as we will not allow others to create fear in us.

There are many things in life that do not submit to our domination and control, and we actually increase our ability to exert our influence over these things when we learn to accept them. This is especially true with respect to the uncertain future. Personal courage does not help us to predict future circumstances, but only how we might meet them. It allows us to trust our ability to respond to the requirements of the moment, and of future moments, regardless of what unfolds. This level of inner courage is displayed by the warrior who says, "I will only die once, when I take my last breath." The coward dies every time he panics. The worrier dies every time he worries. Fear deprives us of life. Courage gives life back. Fear creates chains; courage gives us wings. Rising above our fears is the first step toward creating a fuller, more satisfying life.

CHAPTER ELEVEN

Patience

"There is nothing that does not grow light through habit and familiarity. Putting up with little cares I'll train myself to bear with great adversity." – **Shantideva**

The effective use of patience is often misinterpreted as weakness, indecisiveness, or capitulation. This is surely not so when we are waiting, watching, listening, not reacting to the initial event but instead using our intelligence to decide when and how to give our best response. When we exercise patience, we are not forfeiting something or putting ourselves at a disadvantage. We are actually sharpening our focus and expanding our awareness just when they are needed most. Patience is the antidote to the mind's sense of insecurity and fear. This state of mind allows us to wait, to watch, and to listen. It accommodates a more mature overview of our alternatives and the potential effects each choice may have. It also helps us to remember that many things can only unfold in their own time.

Whenever we are feeling the effects of our negative emotions, patience can create the additional awareness and psychological space needed to better recognize what is happening within us as well as around us. Our minds can be less cluttered with worrisome thoughts. We can feel more at ease in the reality of the present; more alert and discerning and less susceptible to the influences of fear, frustration or anger. Even if others around us are having negative emotional reactions, we can be confident in knowing that we have the freedom to avoid getting swept up in their storms. Thus, patience feeds both equanimity and wisdom.

To better understand this point, we need only observe how often impatience is at the root of worry, fear, anger, discouragement, and failure. Adversity is a condition of life that cannot always be avoided and the suffering it brings is something we must learn to struggle through. For the sake of our own ability to meet our needs and the needs of others, we should want to assure that our struggles have warming, not chilling, effects, and that they expand rather than narrow our foresight wisdom to recognize what choices are available, and where those choices lead. People who might affect us negatively will always be coming and going. Once we accept this, we see that the root cause of our agitation is not in them but in us. If we really want our inner state to be joyful, we cannot afford to place the responsibility for that outcome in the hands of others.

Whenever we feel upset that someone has caused us harm, it is often difficult to step back and examine whether our greater enemy is the external event or the internal condition we are experiencing. If we are operating with sufficient patience to pose this question to ourselves, the very consideration of the question will offer us an essential choice. Wise people will want to know if they are exerting their energy against the right enemy or the wrong enemy, if they are fighting for a good cause or a bad cause. Battling the external enemy is almost always fruitless, though it is initially the most tempting strategy. Patience helps us realize that most things we call problems are experienced as such because we are resisting circumstances that should either be faced or simply let go.

Anger is the precursor to hatred, while patience is the precursor to greater understanding. The toxic feelings and disturbing thoughts that accompany anger can be a persistent source of misery. If life is an inevitable struggle, then let us struggle to increase our patience. In so doing we will also be feeding the processes that increase our levels of confidence, decisiveness, intelligence, and happiness. We will then find ourselves being less bothered by what other people do, because we will be quicker to recognize what a waste of precious energy it is to participate in other people's dramas. This realization is most helpful when it does not arise from a sense of superiority, but rather from an overall view of life that is simply non-threatening.

There are no greater self-imposed transgressions against our own well being than anger and hatred, and there is no greater determinant to our deep and abiding peace of mind than patience. That is why the more patience we develop, the less vulnerable we are to being hurt. The patient predisposition will not actively attract the causes of hurt and even when those causes are near, there will be a greater freedom to avoid the negativity they invite. We will see that it is folly to punish ourselves because somebody else is being foolish or insensitive. We will also be aware that the effect others have on us depends to a great extent on whether our own attitude is to make a situation harmful or helpful. If our desire is to be helpful then each circumstance we encounter becomes the perfect opportunity to make things better, to learn a new lesson, or to achieve well-being.

As we learn to patiently let things take their natural course, we show a trust in life itself. We can relax and allow ourselves to be at ease in the reality of the present; in so doing we come to realize that a sense of ease is the foundation of both happiness and intelligence. If we know how to relax and pay attention in the midst of all that is going on, we will be freer to embrace the tensions and adapt to the changes as they come. The world will teach us what we need to know.

The agitated mind worries too often about how we will get from here to there. Patience operates more realistically by bringing us from there back to here, which is where we are most likely to make the greatest difference.

CHAPTER TWELVE
Uncertainty

"One of the things that has happened to us...as a human race, is to learn how certainty crumbles in your hand. We cannot any longer have a fixed certain view of anything...[but] our lives teach us who we are." – **Salman Rushdie**

Sometimes what we fear most is not knowing how things will turn out, not knowing if we will fail or succeed. Of course, the pressure we feel only increases when we demand certainty from a future that cannot deliver it. Everyone needs some degree of structure and predictability in order to function intelligently, but too much of either can actually weaken the life energy that stimulates our sense of adventure. For many people, uncertainty represents a threatening lack of personal control. Yet the reality of uncertainty highlights that what we make of our lives is more about the conditions within us than the conditions that surround us. The way we learn to truly trust ourselves is to accept this uncertainty as we work our way forward without all the answers.

When we are realistic, we see that we can only be partially aware of our circumstances, or of what lies ahead. We also see that the very essence of a stimulating experience is to embark on a journey for which the outcome is unknown. Often, the achievements we are most proud of are those we created from the unexpected, those that developed in the midst of the kind of drama that only uncertainty can generate. "What shall I do next?" can be a most invigorating question. But for individuals who do not want to take a step forward until they see assurances ahead, this question can be disabling.

All change requires something to be lost; but through change, something better can be gained. As we come to recognize the major historical patterns in life, we see that everything is breaking down: religion, politics, economics, social customs, art, and human relationships; but everything is also building up again in new and different ways. Eventually, these new ways will break down too; the world will change again and again. This constant flux tends to leave those who deny or resist the reality of perpetual change annoyed or worried; but those who understand and accept change are likely to derive happiness, energy, and real satisfaction from the same course of experiences.

There are many conditions in life that we cannot control, yet part of our fate is that we are creative. With each succession of experiences, we will always have choices if we look for them. Those who embrace this attitude believe that as they move forward, new ideas and alternatives will inevitably appear on their mental horizons. They are continuously on the lookout for the open space of opportunity where there will be more to discover, to understand, to be, to do, and to give. The essence of this perspective is captured in a line from Robert Frost's poem "The Road Not Taken." Standing at the point where the road diverges into two, the traveler wonders which road is the better one to take. But then realizing, "how way leads on to way," he is confidently prepared to choose either.

Uncertainty, if approached with this kind of "inner knowing," should induce a sense of freedom—not paralysis. Every action we take from the basis of a positive inner confidence raises the prospect of new powers. To the creative and opportunistic mind, a future that is unpredictable is a future that is wide open. On the other hand, if we mentally resist uncertainty, our resistance will turn into fear. We will feel threatened and more inclined to retreat whenever we reach the edge of what is familiar. Our comfort zones will become places of confinement rather than ports of embarkation.

Those who lack a deep sense of adventure and who function with a considerable need for certainty are often saddled with self-imposed limitations during highly competitive or rapidly changing times. Their energy and efforts will more likely be directed toward identifying and avoiding risky situations. They will search for security, which is nowhere possible because life exists as insecurity, danger, and risk. That is why most first-rate opportunities come in the form of challenges to move *toward*—not away—from risk and uncertainty.

Life is not a race nor a contest, but rather a process of growth. Within this process there is great potential for feeling joy and excitement. We can derive much pleasure simply from looking back to the yesterdays and the day-before-yesterdays and realizing how little we knew before and how far we've progressed. In so doing, we begin to uncover a pattern of evidence indicating that the whole advance of growth is actually driven by uncertainty. Every moment represents something distinct and original in Nature and each unique set of circumstances calls for a fresh understanding and often an original response.

When we learn to approach the uncertain future with a self-assured restlessness and positive goals, instead of false confidence or a fear of the unknown, we find that it is far more stimulating to be an active creator than a passive risk avoider. It is also wiser to allow room in our minds for not always knowing what leads to what. We do better to improve our ability to figure things out along the way. The mind is no exception to the rule of all living things. It must work to keep alive, absorbing the world around it and transforming that world into its own expanding intelligence. Motion is more natural to life than non-motion, and things that keep moving and unfolding are inherently good.

CHAPTER THIRTEEN
Relentless Optimism

"In the depth of winter, I finally learned that there was in me an invincible summer." – **Albert Camus**

Success is quite often not about how to play a good hand, but rather how to play a bad hand well. The world is a powerful conditioner towards negativity, especially when circumstances seem to be working against our most important goals. Pessimism seems to be the typical response, and optimism is atypical—even though our problems are best addressed by a positive attitude. There are times in life when we find ourselves in a dire situation, one that necessitates a deep sense of urgency and requires us to come charging back aggressively and tenaciously if we are to prevail.

Unfortunately, this kind of intense reaction very often expresses itself through negative emotions like anger or resentment and is thus more likely to be ineffective or counter-productive. Relentless optimism offers a response to adversity that can be both highly aggressive and stubbornly positive. This is an attitude that has the capacity to profoundly affect the present moment in advantageous ways. People who learn to be relentlessly optimistic enable themselves to be as motivated by their setbacks as they are by their accomplishments.

Relentless optimism is not about tricking the mind into thinking that everything is good, nor is it the same as wishfully thinking that things will improve on their own. Rather, it is an attitude that helps us to see exactly how things are, in terms of the difficulties and opportunities before us, and the goals we care about most. It is also a statement to ourselves and others that we are neither quitting nor turning back; instead, we are determined to create the optimal results from whatever is happening. We empower that which we focus on, therefore, why not empower our opportunities by shifting our attention to the things that can help us make the best of every situation? Each time we practice this kind of self-responsibility we become more self-determining.

It is largely up to us whether the circumstances we encounter are experienced as opportunity or stress. Our response defines the difference, and whenever life affords us a chance to choose our responses we do well to hold ourselves accountable for what eventuates. To some, this realm of choice is embraced as a freedom, while to others it is perceived as a burden, and resisted. The paradox is that those who resist taking an active role in transforming the negative context of their lives into constructive action and positive meaning will only be setting themselves up to experience more disappointment and suffering from life's issues. In short, they will get less of what they do want and more of what they don't want.

People who possess relentless optimism display a whole-hearted sense of acceptance in the face of difficulties, believing the purpose of life is to go forward. They use life's hardships to wake themselves up rather than to put themselves to sleep. They know that even under the most distressing or constraining circumstances they can find sufficient ways to exercise the independence and power to be self-defining, self-determining. They do not merely cope or survive under duress but instead they consciously decide how they will put forth the best in themselves in *this* moment and what they will make of the next moment. They don't endure, they express. Enduring is more about self-protection. It is a perspective that inhibits. Expressing, however, is proactive and creative. It gives us the freedom to make the best out of the worst, to bring the most from the least.

Relentless optimism requires a deeper, more personal, and ennobling definition of success, a definition based on the premise that life is a journey, not an event. It requires us to subscribe to the proposition that reaching our potential is more important than reaching our goals. This is responsible thinking at its best. This is also indomitable character. It rests on the faith that the intellect, in combination with the human spirit, is at all times capable of transforming the most threatening or disappointing conditions into a constructive, inspiring, and life-advancing force. This force begins exactly at the point where we make the unequivocal commitment to succeed from *here*, wherever *here* might happen to be.

CHAPTER FOURTEEN
Sadness

"Man could not live if he were entirely impervious to sadness. Many sorrows can be endured only by being embraced, and the pleasure taken in them naturally has a somewhat melancholy character." – **Emile Durkheim**

One of the more painful emotions that can actually be utilized for raising our level of consciousness is sadness. Sadness or sorrow should not be something we merely try to survive, outlast, or forget, nor are we wise to inflame its negative side with thoughts of anger, hate, or self-pity. Sadness is a basic feature of life and will always be near. Putting too much effort into avoiding sadness can become a source of greater unhappiness; actively resisting sadness moves us toward depression. We suffer most from sadness when we believe that we shouldn't have to experience it at all. This belief, in and of itself, predisposes the mind to hardship.

Enthusiasm and joy may expand us, but the pain of sadness encourages the development of our spiritual and intellectual depth. In fact, in the midst of the acceptance of sadness, we may already experience the beginning of greater self-awareness and self-understanding. Profound sadness can be purifying, when we allow it to slow us down, humble us, deepen us, and teach us to be more empathic toward others who are undergoing hardships. If we allow ourselves to turn sadness into compassion, healing power can be found in the tenderness of the pain itself. We discover that deep within us there is a sanctum of tranquility and wisdom from which all emotions are transmutable and all experiences can be made useful going forward.

To truly enjoy the peak experiences in life, we must accept that there are also valleys of hurt, sorrow, and disappointment. Pleasure cannot exist without pain, and life cannot exist without death. Life will always be experienced between these polarities and we must be willing to live with the tension that will inevitably be felt. If we try to deny the tension or refuse to accept it, then we will surely suffer from it. Growth requires that we face the reality of our challenges and encounter them—whatever they are. Just as the accomplished sailor knows how to use the wind—regardless of its direction—to go where he wants to go, we can learn to convert the inherent power of our greatest disappointments and hurts into love, appreciation, compassion, and other positive emotions. We can be freer to flow with whatever is happening while having greater trust in life and less fear of it.

When misfortune befalls us, the sympathy we receive from others can provide a very soothing consolation, and can often help us recover more quickly. Unfortunately, some people do not use the sympathy they receive from others to get stronger, but only to feel better. They consume it like junk food. It has no real emotional nourishment. Their feeling of sadness or emptiness comes back very quickly and nothing gets accomplished in the meantime. Like a good medicine, we should only look for sympathy in small doses and not become addicted to the medicine itself. Doing the work of strengthening our minds is far more important than simply making the effort to avoid the pain.

When we allow our sadness to flow freely, we are actually cooperating with what is true of our inner being, that is, that sorrow is endemic to life. When we are deeply sad, we can become more closely aligned to the feelings of love, gratitude and even humor. When we resist sadness, we are more predisposed to weakness and negativity. Then we are more likely to feel anger, hatred, jealousy, and regret. Therefore, it is important to remember that if we are feeling these negative emotions coming from our sadness, then we must be doing something to actively push ourselves away from the blessings of love. Once we learn this lesson, we will be better with sadness when it inevitably arrives.

Sadness is an inescapable part of life. If we cannot be open to sadness, we cannot be open to life. The state of inner resistance will always cause more negativity and make it seem as if life is working against us while the state of inner openness gives us a better chance to be aware and steady under all circumstances. This is not to say that openness will protect us from the pain of sadness. It will only help us avoid the additional and unnecessary suffering that comes from resisting the pain.

If we know how it is to live through our hearts, we will surely come to know what it is to feel our hearts break. It is up to each of us to prove that a broken heart can have great value. When we are willing to examine our sadness honestly and trace its causes to their roots, it is possible to discover a deeper level of the mind that is beyond sadness, beyond all the layers of self protection we've work so hard to create. From this place, we will feel more balanced and still, and our responses to life will naturally move us in the direction of love, joy, kindness, and appreciation.

CHAPTER FIFTEEN
Affirmation(s)

"Kind words can be short and easy to speak, but their echoes are truly endless." – **Mother Teresa**

Simply put, affirmations are positive statements that generate positive energy. The best affirmations encourage and provide earnest assurance of a person's capabilities. There is no better way to motivate others than to open their eyes to their own potential. When people gain a realistic assessment of their own strengths, they begin to see more possibilities for their own success. Therefore, every time we validate another person's positive qualities we are encouraging him or her to put even more energy into expressing those qualities. We are opening the gates to allow those winning elements to flow more freely.

Human beings are not emotionally designed to be islands. At our core, we are interpersonal and interdependent organisms who need to be deeply invested in each other. None of us could have survived our infancy and childhood years if this were not so. Even in adulthood, interdependency continues to be a basic truth of our existence. As we grow older and hopefully become increasingly involved in the pursuit of our individual potential, we will become even more aware that it is better not to go it alone. Whatever we have or feel that brings us joy, peace, and happiness, will only be expanded when we grasp the fundamental principle that these things must be experienced with others before they are fully felt.

Everyone needs affirmation—not just those who have low self esteem. One of the best ways to take possession of our own power in this regard is to practice giving what we need. When we affirm someone else, we elevate ourselves. Personal and professional status may be measured by how many other people one controls but our own psychological growth will be marked by how many others we encourage and inspire. We all thrive more with happy and supportive people in our lives. If we give what we need, what we need will be more available to us. This effect is not so much transactional as it is trans-psychological. This is how we discover how closely our own nature is interrelated with the nature of those with whom we have contact. Outwardly we may rely on simple reciprocity but inwardly we are sharing much of the same energy. What we affirm in others we are affirming and reinforcing in ourselves.

The ability to see good in others starts when we learn to put trust in our own goodness. Our sense of inner confidence cannot be well established until we develop a deep and loving belief in ourselves, even as we humbly admit that we are works in progress. If we feel secure in our aspiration to strive toward becoming all that we have the potential to be, we will not be inclined to abandon our challenges too soon or to look for something easier and safer. As we begin to see the value and the power of affirming ourselves, this positive energy will start to flow outward. This is how a true sense of self worth engenders respect for others.

An affirmation is most useful when it is given by an individual who has enough self-confidence to allow him or her to grant others permission to feel greater self confidence too. Sometimes it takes someone else whom we respect to say, "Yes, you can do this!" to make us reach for our dreams.

The good effects that come from affirming others do not have to be promoted or governed by moral tenets. They do not even need to be end-oriented. Affirmation of another is an end unto itself. By sharing our good feelings, we raise our sense of fulfillment.

CHAPTER SIXTEEN
Lightheartedness

"...let these be your desires: To melt and be like a
running brook that sings its melody to the night. To know the
pain of too much tenderness. To be wounded by your own
understanding of love; and to bleed willingly and joyfully.
To wake at dawn with a winged heart and give thanks for an-
other day of loving" – **Khalil Gibran**

Lightheartedness is a state of being where our relationship with
life itself is relaxed, open, playful, and non-defensive. When we
strive to keep a light heart, happiness naturally shines through
our every experience. This is what makes lightheartedness so
incompatible with tension, anxiety, anger, and discouragement.
Lightheartedness gives us the freedom to face ourselves, and
even more importantly, it helps us to be our best selves. When
we feel free to be who we are, we are unlikely to remain as we
are. As the heart and mind become more cheerful, optimistic,

and hopeful, we are more inclined to make positive changes, and to face the risks required to grow toward our higher potential.

Many who live with heavy hearts believe that lightheartedness can only be sustained by a lack of realism; that only a fool or a dreamer would be consistently happy in a world full of trouble and unrest. But the beauty of lightheartedness is that it does not distort our view of the real world or its predicaments. It is not a vacation from reality. We can be fully aware that life brings suffering, yet also know that when pain, illness, or sadness comes, the lighter heart is a more courageous, compassionate, and resilient heart.

Good relationships do not always last, but the lighthearted person will avoid putting energy into having enemies or being an enemy. Lightheartedness is an outlook that does not harbor any vested need for anger or resentment, because it helps us to be highly aware of the consequences of anger and resentment when these feelings come. With this awareness, we can have negative feelings but they will not grow strong or survive too long in us because our understanding prevents us from feeding them.

Lightheartedness provides very fertile ground for positive emotions, but gives little support to negativity. It allows us to feel and to flow with whatever is happening, and to experience our most difficult challenges as part of the graceful dance we are choreographing with existence. And if we recognize the wisdom and power of this perspective it can only be because we already know what it is to endure and grow through personal hardships. No matter how trying life may be at any given moment, the state of lightheartedness can always guide us back to joy, appreciation, and positive meaning.

Through lightheartedness we experience the preciousness of seemingly simple things, because of our strong sense of being grateful, of being lucky. In this state of mind, we have the ability to see ourselves as we really are and to come back to ourselves regardless of what is happening around us. We are more ready to listen and more able to hear. Even when we are alone, we seldom feel lonely. We trust in the basic creativity and fullness of life itself, and we are empowered in any situation, with endless ways of doing what we want to do and being who we want to be. We never have to imitate. If we adopt best practices from others, it is because those practices appeal to us and we want to draw them into our repertoire of behaviors.

The ability to cultivate lightheartedness intentionally adds another dimension of freedom to our life. There is no need to ever feel trapped in our circumstances. There is a deeply felt unity between our inner observer and that which is being observed. There is something about us that remains unaffected by transient circumstances going on around us, and we cannot be fundamentally disturbed by fluctuating conditions. We can be aware of them, respond to them, enjoy them, sharpen our skills, and even create meaning through them, but there will be no need to over-attach ourselves to them. In the state of lightheartedness, we realize that the environment is not what matters most, but the extent to which we are in harmony with it.

CHAPTER SEVENTEEN
Restlessness and Movement

"Even if all these other needs are satisfied, we may still
often, if not always, expect that a new discontent and
restlessness will soon develop, unless the individual is doing
what he is fitted for. A musician must make music, an artist
must paint." – **Abraham Maslow**

A well-balanced mind contains both restlessness and contentment. In fact, each arises out of the other. Restlessness
is essential to our natural development. It is the surface tension rising from a deep-rooted feeling that there is something higher and better than our present selves. Everything we
have achieved up to this point is only a seed for what we can
eventually become. What we are actually feeling is the energy
contained in what is ready to emerge next, the fault line of
shifting energy between being and becoming. As Robert
Browning wrote, "Our aspirations are our possibilities." How

could we ever find the strength to evolve if not for the zeal that restlessness contains?

A human being is a creative process, an organism expressing the fundamental creativity of the world. When we look at human nature, we see that it is based on transformation. Each of us has a unique blueprint for growth, what Plato called the *divine design*, and we experience this design continuously through our feelings. Its signals are conveyed in the form of our passions and interests, but also through our anxieties and disenchantments. The more we become attuned to these inner urgings, the more we will be driven to move, search, seek new challenges, and bring forth greater fulfillment from every stage of life. We can only be in growth mode if we are on the move, for becoming is our nature. The moment we believe we are complete, we stop evolving.

Our relationship with restlessness can be positive if it is accompanied by patience and intelligence. It is usually easier to run away from tension or agitation, but avoidance is rarely helpful. Sometimes it is far more beneficial to connect with our restlessness while seeking to discover what our inner world is trying to convey. These signals of our deeper intelligence, which are expressed in our desires, yearnings, and other impulsive signals, are coming from the life force within us. They are compatible with our nature rather than being opposed to it. Any responsible attempt to fully define human beings must include our instinctive drives to develop physically, mentally, emotionally, and spiritually according to the codes of our genetic blueprint. If we come to accept our feelings of restlessness as less of a struggle and more of a call to channel our energy in positive ways, we will avoid the obstacles of negative thinking, which only inhibit our adaptive abilities.

The nagging sense that we want more than we have can be of value. It is a sign of things changing within us, the drumbeat of our instinctual human drives. Yet problems arise when we follow this restlessness only in the material realm. When our progress in the outer world outweighs that of the inner world, we will experience that imbalance as a feeling of emptiness. Even if we deny the importance of the inner life, we cannot escape our inner needs.

Life is a highly dynamic process; it can never be static. Einstein acknowledged this when he said, "Nothing happens until something moves." With movement, life is stirred and energy begins to flow. The challenge for us is how to maintain our balance with it—or perhaps we should refer to this phenomenon with a verb: *balancing*. Balancing is something that happens naturally as we learn to openly face and examine uneasiness and to adapt to our realities. A human being is composed of many different dimensions and we will suffer if we allow these dimensions to be in conflict with each other. For example, if we are deeply satisfied for too long, our growth energy will slow down dramatically. The good life cannot be a continuous state of tranquility and satisfaction. The feeling of contentment, when it is achieved through healthy means, will inevitably give way to a desire to become active again, to do more changing and growing. This desire may come in the form of ambition or perhaps a strong sense of lacking. Either way, we will become restless for a new challenge or even problem. When this kind of restlessness comes, we do well to expect it, embrace it, and most of all trust its value.

Life will continually flow through us, taking us from harmony to disharmony and on to more mature forms of harmony. Our higher goal is to keep experiencing these changes as opportunities for transformation, having faith that whatever eventuates from our periods of unsettledness will be useful as long as we are using them to work our way forward. In this way, we experience the seemingly contradictory state of being highly alert and active while simultaneously learning what is required to relax into whatever is going on. Eventually, we come to understand how restlessness and movement are fundamental and complimentary principles of reality. Harmony can only be achieved while the music is playing.

CHAPTER EIGHTEEN
Relaxation

"Besides the noble art of getting things done, there is a nobler art of leaving things undone. The wisdom of life consists in the elimination of the nonessentials." – **Lin Yutang**

The modern world is geared primarily for work, not psychological growth. By the time we reach adulthood, many of us are thoroughly conditioned to be hyperactive and to worship speed, ambition, efficiency, and productivity. Unfortunately, we may know very little about the benefits of resting, relaxing, and generally doing less. Many forms of rest and relaxation are disparaged as idleness and this is perhaps because we've been taught to look at relaxation as "down time," or as simply being unproductive. We may worry that spending too much of our lives in this down time will cause us to become lazy or sluggish and to fall farther behind in the ostensibly competitive pursuits of happiness and prosperity.

Underlying these beliefs there is a vague yet pervasive feeling in our society that we are in a race to reach somewhere, though we seldom have the time, or just don't use our time to contemplate exactly where that somewhere is. Instead, there is a general sense in many that the key to getting there is to go faster. We read many books on success that teach ways to effectively get more things done more quickly; this kind of advice only feeds our misunderstanding of reality. As long as we are alive, there will never be an end of things to do. The more fixated we are on *doing*, the more surely our *to do* lists will grow and so too will our tension. Therefore, in terms of finding a greater balance, it is far wiser to look for opportunities to reduce our activities, not increase them.

This is not to say that relaxation is always about doing nothing. It can often be achieved in the midst of being busy simply by shifting into a mindset of acceptance. Life is always sending us problems and putting pressure on us but there is never a time or situation in which the conditions of happiness are not also present. If we want to be more open to these conditions, we must be willing to relax and accept whatever is happening. Whenever we consciously resist what is, we are putting ourselves in a state of inner conflict. We are rejecting part of life—some very personal part—and this is how we become divided against ourselves. Relaxation cannot come unless we allow life to be as it is. If we become agitated over little things, then we should take responsibility for the fact that it is mostly our attitude that agitates us. The more quickly we can recover and are able to accept what is going on around us, the more quickly we will feel ourselves starting to relax; as we relax, we will feel our energy coming back to us. Maybe we will even find that the situation we're in is not as much of a struggle as we were making it out to be.

One way of describing relaxation is that it is the way we feel when stress is absent. Therefore, to enhance our ability to relax, we must learn to become more unreceptive to stress. It is foolish to increase our tolerance for it. If we learn to take more we can expect to attract more, because all we have done is reinforced the stress response in ourselves. But if we learn the habit of stepping back from stress and relaxing deeply, even for a few moments, we will find that we are far more effective in our work, our decision-making, and our relationships than we are through the habits of worrying, obsessing, over-planning, or over-controlling.

As we expand and refine our ability to relax, good things will start happening. We will feel less trapped by stressful circumstances. Letting go will become easier, we will begin to place more trust in ourselves, and we will become more adept at drawing power from whatever situation we are in. Harmony, happiness, and health should be what we are aiming to derive from this power. If they are not, we will be more likely to worry, obsess, control, and over-manipulate things and people. It will be far more difficult to cooperate with our circumstances because we will be expecting our circumstances to align with our demands. Life for us will have a very narrow set of acceptable conditions and we will hold an antagonistic attitude toward all non-conforming conditions. This is a state of mind familiar to all of us, it is called unhappiness.

It is entirely possible for us to create a synergistic relationship between working hard and relaxing deeply. It requires being willing to work hard some of the time so that we can relax at other times. If we cannot do both, our positive energy will be undermined in the long run. Too much relaxation or contentment becomes a kind of death. Contentment, at its best, will occur only intermittently, but we can expect from it a healthy desire to get going again, to pursue challenging and meaningful goals. A human being needs to want. We must have desires in order to be motivated, but what we desire most is our own happiness. In terms of the interplay between restlessness and relaxation, happiness is cultivated when we can move intelligently and smoothly between being happily stimulated and happily content.

CHAPTER NINETEEN
Vulnerability

"When we were children, we used to think that when
we were grown-up we would no longer be vulnerable.
But to grow up is to accept vulnerability... To be alive is to
be vulnerable." – **Madeleine L'Engle**

Until we acknowledge our vulnerability, we cannot begin to really live. If we allow ourselves to be too afraid of life's risks we will struggle to know our full potential and most likely spend the majority of our time in protection mode. Mental and emotional equilibrium do not exist as a steady and secure state. There will always be problems and these can be faced, but the excessive need to safeguard ourselves against risk is a problem that is very difficult to overcome. The source of emotional security is not without but within. Insecurity is the essential nature of the outer world. That is why wisdom has less to do with holding onto control and more to do with letting go.

Life is in constant motion and we do well to keep moving with it. The human being cannot avoid the role of human doing, human risking as a being in action. The ongoing challenge, therefore, is to keep balancing, which involves losing our balance and then finding it again, tipping toward one side and then toward the other, sometimes falling but always getting back up again. Even our mistakes should be teaching us a great deal about who we are. In order to find the right door, we will need to go through many wrong doors. This is how effective growth proceeds.

The moments we choose to say, "I can flow with the way things are," we have accepted our vulnerability, and by this we have accepted life's genuine conditions. Then we are truly ready to join with life and be in synchrony with its rhythms. We can exercise the freedom to navigate our journeys from the inside out, to let our experiences transform us and teach us what we are ready to learn next. If our inner growth remains a higher priority, nothing can dominate us—at least not for very long. Life puts no boundaries on our ability to be ourselves.

Sometimes, when faced with an important decision, we can become stressed by the belief that there is one absolute best option, and if we do not select *correctly* we will ruin our greatest chance for success. Fortunately, that is seldom true. There is much about our existence that we cannot control or foresee, and there are days when we can feel like the proverbial straw in the wind of circumstances. But while the inert piece of straw is powerless to set its own course, human beings are born with the ability to perceive, to imagine, to choose among options, and to adjust intelligently to the consequences of our choices.

There are many promising potentialities waiting to happen in our lives, but if we are too occupied with security issues we will not take the risks needed for these potentialities to manifest. We do better by trusting that life will send us the lessons we need to learn when we are ready to learn them. If we are having a difficult experience, we profit by taking the opportunity to learn from it. It is foolhardy to think that we can learn what we need to learn only when things are going smoothly, or when we are in control of all the variables. Any situation in which control is lost may look like danger to the security-minded person, even though in most instances our sense of control is an illusion.

We protect ourselves internally through our emotional defense mechanisms such as worry, jealousy, resentment, and anger, and of course fear, but these defenses are most appropriate to the earlier stages of our development. In the metaphor of the seed and its shell, the shell is needed to give the seed protection, but if the shell covers the seed for too long, the seed will die. The seed cannot become begin to sprout until it leaves the protection of the shell and merges with the soil.

The point is this: we cannot know what we have the potential to become, and we will not find out, unless we have the courage to accept vulnerability by letting go of our favorite defenses. It is impossible to be consciously aware of life's "true" conditions and yet continue to have lots of worries. How can we live like we are a significant part of a unified whole, or learn to cooperate with life's changes, if we are harboring the feeling that the world is conspiring against us?

Vulnerability means living without the false armor of worry, jealousy, resentment, and anger. Growing toward our higher selves requires us to be willing to feel the fear that comes with living dangerously. If we can let go of our favorite defenses and allow our fear to flow freely, it may grow so intense that we will eventually have to let go of that, too. We will have to rely on courage, intelligence, and patience instead. Then we will truly begin to see what we are made of. Then we will come to understand that regardless of whatever may seem to be falling apart, we create our situations mostly by how we use our minds. Have we ever stopped to ask ourselves what would happen if everything we cling to fell apart but our happiness?

CHAPTER TWENTY
Resilience

*"Our greatest glory is not in never falling, but rising every time
we fall."* – **Confucius**

Mental and emotional well-being is not based on invulnerability
or impenetrability, but rather on resilience, which is the internal
strength to mount a formidable comeback after every setback.
At the level of day-to-day living everyone fails sooner or later,
and every achievement eventually runs its course. Thus the willingness to risk failure and endure its consequences whenever
necessary is another crucial element to our self-development.

Giving ourselves permission to fail or to suffer a setback should
we have to can actually enhance our chances for success—not
by encouraging failure but rather by allowing us to drop our
fear of it. Unfortunately, the inherent value of giving ourselves
the freedom to fail is not widely accepted, and perhaps that is

why we are seldom taught how to fail with dignity, strength, and heightened awareness. Nevertheless, many of life's most valuable lessons cannot be simply told or written, but only experienced directly by those who possess the intelligence and fortitude to learn what it is to get knocked down and get back up again.

If we grow accustomed to giving up too easily, our inner determination will atrophy while our concept of defeat and failure becomes inflated and oversimplified. We will want to avoid challenges and uncertainties whenever possible because any failure might be seen as potentially devastating. Those who have little capacity to take misfortune and disappointment can scarcely afford to risk being exposed to them. Unless we allow our inner resolve to be tested and toughened by life, we severely limit the development of our talents.

On the other hand, each time we pass such a test, we improve our abilities to convert breakdowns into breakthroughs and setbacks into comebacks. There is no better basis for self-confidence than the knowledge that we can endure and grow through life's most difficult tests. Making our way through tough times has less to do with the specific strategies we employ and more to do with our conviction and resolve to face our challenges, deal with them, and move ahead.

There is a significant difference between making a bad experience part of our memory and making it part of our wisdom. When trouble is merely retained in memory, it may be perceived as yet another of life's wounds that may heal over time, but only to leave another scar, another weak spot, a reminder that life will surely injure and hurt us. When memory is allowed to play the predominant role, it will place the greatest importance on the past, not the future. Memory prefers to work with prudence and caution. It focuses best on the prevention of future injuries and, therefore, stands ready to remind us of the risks. Memory is fundamentally rational and logical. It likes to collect additional pieces to what we already know, while wisdom has the intuitive power to create new schemas for re-organizing and re-envisioning ways to optimize what we learn from each experience.

Wisdom operates from a deeper level of knowing. When wisdom takes the lead, memory plays the role of the good servant—and that is when memory is most helpful. Wisdom is always searching for a better way forward. When a bad experience is incorporated into wisdom, the injurious effects are only experienced briefly before they are channeled into our larger reservoir of understanding. Memory may reverberate with a hundred echoes of a negative experience while wisdom may discern a thousand fresh insights from the same situation.

Whenever we are looking back at negative memories we should probably ask, "Do we want past wounds to become part of our inner fear or our inner balance?" We know that we are totally free from past wounds when we no longer resent them, when we don't harbor long term grudges or complaints. It is possible to carry many scars but not be haunted by them. Scars need not automatically inflict emotional damage on us. Instead, they can support our wisdom by reminding us of past wounds that have healed. They can serve as emblems of our resilience.

The Buddhists use the analogy of two arrows to explain this theory. The first arrow to strike us represents the event, the initial adversity that comes our way. It has already occurred and we cannot avoid it. The second arrow is our negative reaction to the first arrow. If we examine closely the effects of the second arrow, we see that it is more damaging and brings us far more suffering than the first. The second arrow is also more unfortunate because we shoot it into ourselves, sometimes over and over, and yet we will blame someone else for the suffering it causes us. The second arrow adds to and complicates the initial pain and yet it is optional. When we choose to shoot the second arrow it keeps us in a state of anger or fear. As long as we keep our focus on the second arrow we will miss the opportunity to learn from the experience of the first arrow.

The second arrow is always about our confusion. In the absence of confusion, it is possible to find freedom, joy, and positive meaning even in the presence of the first arrow. This growth is not accomplished by practicing denial, or being indifferent to the pain brought by the first arrow. Rather, it requires us to face the initial problem, and to study it until we understand it to its roots. There we will find our misery is only a state of mind. At the roots of a negative state of mind so do we also find the roots of a positive state of mind. It is good for us to be familiar with both. If we lived in a perfect world, we would quite simply stop growing. Emotional injury will always be near and will surely work against us when we have little faith in our ability to deal with it. Even when there is no way out of our miserable circumstances, there is usually a way through.

CHAPTER TWENTY–ONE
Being in the Moment

"For the real question is whether the 'brighter future' is really always so distant. What if, on the contrary, it has been here for a long time already, and only our own blindness and weakness has prevented us from seeing it around us and within us, and kept us from developing it?" – **Vaclav Havel**

There is a known and accepted relationship between the moments, the days, and the years of our lives. The conditions that make up this present moment are to a great extent a result of how we have managed past moments. Conversely, what will become of us in the future is being shaped and influenced by the things we are thinking and doing right now. With that in mind, it is best to approach every moment as a creative opportunity to initiate a new and better beginning.

The very effort to be in the moment is not about grasping hold of a particular slice of time, but rather about the quality and range of our awareness during the present time. Should it even matter that we cannot catch hold of each passing moment or make it last longer? The more important point is this: the present moment becomes larger in us when we expand our capacity to see what is there to be seen. The art of being in the present moment is not a time issue, but rather a matter of space and awareness. Our mental astuteness during each present moment exists in proportion to our awareness of where we are and what is happening around us. This determines the difference between minimal and maximal consciousness.

Here, in the present, is the only place we can experience the flow of life, therefore, it is the only time we can learn to cooperate artfully with that flow and avoid living in opposition to it. Life is always moving and changing. Every moment we are opening a new door and facing circumstances that are unique and original. If we rely on past knowledge or preconceived expectations rather than being keenly aware of what is unfolding around us, we may not see how today is different than yesterday. We might as well be machines that are already programmed by the past.

Our understanding of all we have learned previously should be refined on an ongoing basis as we continuously integrate what we already know with what we are presently experiencing. Life does not stop teaching and intelligence is not meant to be static. It requires the ability to remain an open process, to see what new things are happening, and to be in harmony with changes so as to avoid becoming fixed in any dogmatic position.

It is important to take our lessons from both the good and the bad that have happened, but when we worry too much about the past, it can needlessly interfere with the quality of the present. This can be so wasteful. Why should we suffer from what is over when it cannot changed? If it is nothing more than a memory, then why continue to give it our energy and thus the power to hurt by replaying it again and again? This will only be useful if we are interested in prolonging our identification with guilt, anger, jealousy, or frustration.

Many people will not allow themselves to let go of their hurts, hates, and grudges. They give their negative memories major ongoing roles in their present attention and then wonder why they remain so miserable. It is wiser to recognize that the past cannot be undone or redone, learn what we can from it, and then move on. We can possess our memories without letting them possess us. We can use them wisely but not allow them to use us foolishly. Right now, at this very moment, by saying yes to what is and accepting what cannot be undone because it already happened, we can shift our focus away from the things we cannot change and act strongly to influence today's situation toward that which is positive.

If we perceive the sources of happiness as outside ourselves or in the future, we will never quite catch up to them, no matter how much hard work we put into reaching them, or how much we think we deserve them. The real source of happiness is always within, and there is no time when it can be experienced other than now. When we maintain the ability to stay in the moment we can decide from moment to moment how we want to experience life. If we are paying attention to the present we can always improve upon it. Unhappiness inevitably arises when we are investing too much thought in past dramas or future worries and fail to realize our existence is taking place now. Happiness knocks on our door each moment and how often do we say, "Not now, I am too busy chasing into the future for the things that will make me happy?"

Tomorrow is merely a concept and perhaps a tremendously helpful one, but it also possesses the qualities of an illusion. When we hold the perspective that tomorrow is something that exists objectively, we give it the power to deceive us. The past no longer is, while the future is not yet, but the biggest difference between the two is that the past really did happen. It was at one time an actual present experience and many aspects of it remain in our minds through our accumulated memories. Whatever might have happened in the past is only advantageous if it helps us to be at home in the present. The future is trickier because it is only a mental projection based on what is not yet real. Thoughts of the future can disturb our mind with things and events that never were and may never be. Just as it is unwise to suffer from what is over, it is equally unwise to suffer from what has not yet happened. The wise person is peripherally aware of past and future but his or her main focus is on the present.

Being happy in the moment is not about gaining the power to control, but giving ourselves the freedom to let go. It is a matter of being so centered and balanced on the inside that we can feel secure even as we accept that many of the outside variables that influence our life remain uncontrollable. It is about enjoying a sense of well-being because we are aware and grateful for what we have. If we put our efforts into maintaining the quality of our inner presence, and then operate from there, we can aspire to make all of our responses a reflection of our truest strengths rather than our deepest fears. What we do with our choices today will shape the causes of tomorrow's effects. Imagine the effects of living our whole life making every moment and every phase of it a joy, a beauty, and a reward. If we learn how to take care of the minutes, the hours will take care of themselves.

CHAPTER TWENTY–TWO
Humility

"Pride makes us artificial and humility makes us real."
—**Thomas Merton**

Genuine humility is a state of mind produced when balanced intelligence combines with realistic self-esteem. The lack of humility usually indicates that our mind is in a state of ignorance. Humility may not be a primary cause of psychological well-being, but it is surely a signal of it and the two accompany each other with great regularity. Once the spirit of humility is deeply internalized, it need not be encouraged or coached. It will arise in our demeanor quite naturally as we cultivate other qualities such as respect, dignity, kindness, and love. Thoughts and actions that ensue from humility carry greater emotional and intellectual capital when they are not mandated by ethical or moral authority. Humility is best motivated by an inner imperative and an understanding that we are all in this life together. The realization that we are a part of everything is in itself very humbling.

If we acquire humility in this way, we do not forsake our most important personal interests. Rather we open ourselves up to many vital advantages. We can expect to be happier, more aware, and more adaptive to life's demands. Our hearts will feel lighter because we are not weighed down by the distortions of pride, vanity, and arrogance. We will be more effective at meeting our higher needs and the needs of others. We will be less prone to responding too aggressively or too submissively. Our deference toward others will reflect a sense of belonging—not insecurity. It will convey trust—not fear, self-confidence—not timidity, and indebtedness—not greed. The value of every experience will be elevated as we increase our capacity to appreciate again and again the daily conditions of life.

Humility mitigates our negative feelings because it helps us to see that everything that happens in life, especially our difficulties, can serve a positive purpose, even if we do not immediately understand what that purpose might be. This can promote the kind of acceptance that is far from capitulation or passive resignation. Instead, it is a more intelligent form of acceptance that remains focused on issues of higher consciousness and spiritual growth. In effect, we feel positive and willing to flow with whatever is happening because we do not consider this a manner of giving in but of moving up. Therefore, there is little interest in taking any position that increases strife, conflict, vanity, or upset. When humility permeates our frame of mind we see that our true self-interests are better served by seeking lovingness, compassion, simplicity, and peacefulness. Humble people have little need for enemies.

There are times when vanity and arrogance may make us feel more powerful, but in the long term they leave us weak. When we suffer from excess pride, we are limited in our ability to enjoy the gift of appreciation and gratitude. This limitation comes from the erroneous belief that we are chiefly responsible for our blessings. When we are feeling arrogant or conceited we cannot experience the pleasure that comes from respecting something greater than ourselves. We do well to study the power of genuinely humble people. Their humility is a product, or consequence, of a deeper understanding of life and their appropriate place in it. They know how to be an asset to themselves and others. They seem to feel more at home in the universe.

When we think that we are not getting as much as we deserve, we create in ourselves a perspective of deficit and weakness. On the other hand, when we are humble we live in a context of abundance. Our cup runs over and we gain self-confidence. We begin to see our own greatness and we can allow ourselves to reach for it. We are not taking it away from anyone else. It is not even an egocentric desire. Rather, those who have the courage and the will to become themselves often find it easier to focus on the needs of others. Some may misinterpret their ambitions as a sign of arrogance, but even so, the truly humble person gives others implicit permission to misunderstand him or her. He or she will not over-react to them. In any case, it is seldom the business of a humble person to seek the widespread approval of others. He or she knows that it is not necessary to devalue ourselves in order to be humble. We need only refrain from devaluing others.

When we watch ourselves from the stillness of the quiet mind, it is important to assess whether our thoughts and behaviors are concordant with healthy humility. If we discover that they are not, we can assume that we are operating with a distorted sense of reality. We are either taking ourselves too seriously or not seriously enough. But when we learn to embrace life as a precious gift, when we keep in mind that everything we are, and all the blessings we enjoy come from life, we will be genuinely and powerfully humble. In this way, the feelings of gratitude and humility grow out of one another.

CHAPTER TWENTY–THREE
Gratitude

"Gratitude is not only the greatest, but also the parent of all the other virtues." — **Cicero**

The natural human response to being grateful for what one has, or has been given, is the reciprocal desire to be open to the needs of others. That is why relationships thrive wherever gratitude is abundantly present. Gratitude is not just a few thankful words uttered to others, but a deeply enlightened way to live. Feeling grateful for the good things in our lives will automatically increase our sensitivity and receptiveness to the finest benefits each day brings. When we focus on the things for which we are most thankful, we give a gift to ourselves as well as those around us. We are setting into motion a cycle of positive interpersonal dynamics. The more we feel gratitude, the more we come to life.

Does happiness makes us grateful or does gratitude make us happy? The mind is basically neutral. What is right and what is wrong with life seem to exist in parallel realities, but when we focus our attention on what is going well, we become happier. What matters then is how we address this conscious choice. Awareness and the freedom to choose the perspective of gratitude give us the ability to re-contextualize those things we see as problems and to transform them into constructive challenges and opportunities. The sources of our problems are not ignored in this re-contextualization; they are merely judged by a new, more positive perspective. Gratitude is a powerful and healthy state of mind because within it, anger, jealousy, fear, resentment, and frustration cannot co-exist.

When we are grateful, our happiness is not contingent upon expectations that specific blessings should come into our lives. We are motivated instead by a deeply internalized gratitude for the gift of life itself. If something good comes our way, then we feel thankful. If nothing comes then we will still feel grateful, for there was evidently no need for it to come. If we know how to be happy with or without it, then there was surely no necessity for it to come. Happiness will always be more plentiful in a non-demanding state of mind.

The ability to find something to be grateful for in the face of tragedy and misfortune is an indomitable human strength. When we are laid low by a grievous loss, gratitude helps us feel more appreciation for what we have left. If we build upon this perceived interrelationship between the hurt over the loss of something cherished and the heightened awareness of the preciousness of what yet remains, we may even be disposed to give thanks in all situations.

Holding this view, we become unencumbered by the common fears and worries of normal life. We are free to operate from a combination of realism and optimism, believing that when bad things happen they can eventually turn into good things, but when good things happen they rarely turn bad. When gratitude is a dominant theme in all we do, oppositions fade from our life, irritating issues become less relevant, and we learn to gain strength from whatever happens. All experiences become invitations to grow.

Gratitude is the state of mind where generosity is born. Those who are motivated by a generous spirit give much, simply from the inner feeling that they already have much, and they enjoy the giving. They are not sacrificing but sharing what is overflowing in them. They are grateful they can give and grateful that their gifts are accepted. In this way generosity reinforces gratitude and actually creates a broader channel for good things to flow back to us.

Gratitude generates an atmosphere of mutual sharing and starts not when we are asking for something, but rather when we are deeply appreciative for the blessings that have already come to us. We are operating with the feeling we have more than we need—or at least more than we expected. We want to do our own part to continue the benefits of generosity and kindness, which originated from the goodwill of others.

Children feel gratitude for specific things given to them by specific people, but their gratitude is still limited by their narrow perspective. With the mind of a maturing adult, however, our gratitude can take on wiser dimensions according to our broader understanding of life. As the reality we comprehend becomes a larger and more interrelated setting, we are prone to be more generally grateful for all the fine people who have moved into and through our lives and for all the blessings they have shared with us. This leads us to feel more thankful for what we also have to share with others. At this point, our happiness is no longer about what we have, but rather what we enjoy and appreciate. Ultimately, the best way to show our appreciation for being alive is to make a gift of our life by trying to be the best we can be at all times, in all places, and under all conditions.

CHAPTER TWENTY-FOUR
Generosity

*"Thousands of candles can be lit from a single candle, and
the life of the candle will not be shortened. Happiness never
decreases by being shared."* — **Buddha**

As we experience the emotional state of gratitude, we can also
feel its companion motivation, generosity. When we consciously appreciate the conditions of our life, we are more
likely to become involved in activities that promote the well-
being of other people. In fact, the power of generosity cannot
begin to form until we are able to shift our focus away from
needing and instead toward giving. The human spirit naturally blooms when we stop worrying about how to *get* more
and begin placing our emphasis on how to *give* more, how to
give unconditionally.

Human beings are both selfish and collaborative by nature. We have survival needs, individual needs, and most importantly higher needs. When we consider certain people to be selfish in the negative sense, they are most likely focused on fulfilling their lower needs. Their primary motives will be to compensate for what they think they lack. But those we call selfless are more likely to be focused on their higher needs, which is the same as saying they are committed to serving something larger and more important than their own lives. They are familiar with the experience of feeling satisfied and are even comfortable with their dissatisfactions because they know how to channel them into growth.

The elements that contribute to the development of our higher potentials such as love, compassion, and responsibility cannot be acquired by us nor taken from us. They are qualities that grow out of us as we learn to give them, and they naturally lead us toward concern for others. That is why the inclination to give generously is such a powerful human strength. It never diminishes the self, but always expands it. When we are engaged in the pursuit of our higher needs, we find there are more than enough things in life that can bring out our happiness. We are overflowing with joy and appreciation, and we come to find that the more we share these emotional riches, the more they come alive in us.

Many of us would like to be more generous, yet we hold back from giving because we feel that we ourselves do not have enough. There are many things we still need or want before we can afford to be more charitable with others. But this kind of reasoning is just a trick of the mind and keeps us in a state of ignorance about the true nature of happiness. If we identify too strongly with what we have or don't have, our minds will be perpetually troubled. We will already be traveling down the wrong road by equating what we have with who we are. This way of thinking often leads to the perspective that "I don't have enough yet" which actually means, "I am not enough yet." Too much of this kind of wanting will keep unhappiness alive.

If we cannot find satisfaction in what we have, we are not going to find it in what we want. Likewise, if we can't find peace in who we are, how will we find it in who we want to be? As long as we allow these kinds of thought patterns to operate unchallenged in us, no amount of *more* will ever bring us sustainable happiness. We can never get enough of that which we think we need but don't really need.

Generosity does not involve sacrifice—at least not in the common way of seeing sacrifice as a loss. If there is any letting go at all, it is a matter of giving up the lesser for the greater. The result is self-rewarding rather than self-depleting. That is why we should not look for appreciation every time we give generously. If it feels good to give, then do so. Feel the joy in it. If we give to others because we are in dire need of appreciation, we are only setting ourselves up for a letdown. We will be predisposed to disappointment precisely because we are not acting from a spirit of gratitude. We are not sharing but actually transacting with another, using others for what we want in return. This state of mind comes from unhappiness and is almost the direct opposite of generosity. We may try to fool ourselves into believing that we are being generous, but in effect we are being miserly. What we are doing may appear to be giving but deep down it is the act of grasping.

True generosity can only be experienced and expressed in the context of gratitude and self respect, while greed is an expression of fear and emptiness. Those who exude generosity are not needy in the self-limiting sense, but rather they are ambitious to grow in their humanity. They are motivated by their need to develop their gifts for the sake of giving them. And because they feel a greater passion for what they are giving than from what they are receiving, they are much freer to seek harmony with others. They can afford to remain open to the rewards of being alive.

Forgiveness

*"He who cannot forgive breaks the bridge over which
he must pass."* — **George Herbert**

Forgiveness is at times mistaken for weakness, though the pure act itself requires some of our strongest qualities such as honesty, courage, and wisdom. What makes forgiveness especially powerful is that nothing else can relieve us from so much negativity. Forgiveness can wash the toxic emotions like anger, resentment and jealousy from us, thereby allowing our more positive selves to reign. It rekindles the desire and the will to start moving forward again.

Forgiveness is an effective way of truly facing reality and realizing the wisdom of giving up hope for a better past. It does not necessarily mean we are pardoning the wrongs done to us, but it is, to a certain extent, a letting go of our bad feelings about them. Why should anyone continue to suffer from what is over? We all know that we cannot change the past, but that does not always prevent us from the foolishness of getting stuck in it. The wise do not forget the past either, but they are far more interested in what the past might teach them.

It is natural to feel happy when we believe that we have received a significant positive benefit from someone else. By the same token, when we believe someone has done us harm, we feel unhappy. The primary business of the intelligent mind is to expand our ability to be deeply happy. Hence we should work continuously to discover or generate positive advantages from all of our experiences, good or bad. Why should we delay our own progress because of the ill will that others may hold against us, or that we may be harboring against them?

It is more productive to examine each situation critically to see whether or not we have ultimately benefited from the transgression against us. If we see that we are now better off *because* of the experience, because we have transformed that experience to inner growth, what then is the advantage of withholding forgiveness? What debt remains if there is nothing to negate? We may choose to keep clinging to anger and resentment in order to guard against further harm or suffering, but ironically this only invites more harm and suffering into our lives. The ability to forgive is indispensable to enduring happiness.

Forgiveness is a difficult step for the agitated mind to take, because we can become so invested in the antagonistic positions we have chosen. It is too easy to get caught up in self-limiting themes such as right vs. wrong or fair vs. unfair. These are parameters that needlessly put constraints on understanding and awareness, and allow us to become entrenched in the feeling of righteousness. We may be slow to recognize the wiser, more compassionate options available to us because those options are usually beyond the mere understanding of right and wrong.

If we feel a deep generosity for life itself, we will not be inclined to forgive in a self-righteous way. Self-righteousness seldom helps to make contentious matters better. In fact, the words "I forgive you" can often set the *I* and the *you* too far apart from each other for the betterment of either, especially when it implies virtue in the *I* and error in the *you*. The mature person realizes that any sincere act of forgiveness must be, by its very intention, an act of healing.

This is why forgiveness is fundamentally for our own sakes. It provides us with great relief as it releases the mind to live through the power of the heart once again. The heart immediately begins to repair itself when we let go of anger, hatred, and resentment. Forgiveness releases the mind from the prison of the past and brings us back to the power of the present. It brings us back to conscious awareness, and we start improving and re-shaping our circumstance from the inside out.

The healthiest way to forgive is not to let go of our grievances begrudgingly but to analyze them deeply until we see that our own hate or resentment serves no beneficial purpose. The more closely we examine our negativity, the more we will realize our justifications are merely rationalizations and childish excuses that perpetuate our own self-centeredness. Even if other people have wronged us, holding resentments toward them puts us in a very weak and vulnerable state, because the happiness we experience from reducing our resentments is always much greater than the happiness we experience from indulging them. Anytime we have the mindfulness to view our resentments for what they really are, our own sound logic will require that we let them go willingly and happily.

CHAPTER TWENTY-SIX
A Free Self

"'What is the world's greatest lie?' the boy asked. 'It is this: that at a certain point in our lives, we lose control of what's happening to us, and our lives become controlled by fate. That's the world's greatest lie.'" **– Paulo Coelho**

Each human being is inherently unique, something original in Nature, and yet we are undeniably social beings. We have an innate need to belong, to be needed, and even more so, to be cherished by those closest to us. As we grow through childhood and into adulthood, we are strongly motivated to become somebody special in the eyes of others, to make our mark within our social networks through our personal achievements. If we are unselfish, we will want to contribute in some way to the greater good, whether this translates to the betterment of family, community, country, or the world at large. Deep within us, however, there will always linger a compelling desire to know and express our free selves. In social terms it is almost a contradiction. We surrender much of our freedom to the crowd in order to be accepted by the crowd, and then we search for ways to earn back the freedom we crave.

Unfortunately, modern life does little to promote or teach the art of looking inside ourselves. People may become extravagantly wealthy by achieving an in-depth knowledge of how the world of business works, but there are few external reward systems aimed at encouraging self-understanding. This is why, too often, the price we pay for succeeding in the outside world is failure in the inner world. What good does it do to gain power, affluence, and social status if we never attain sovereignty of our own selves? Peace, love, happiness and real security cannot be found in things such as money, power, prestige, or even respectability. Without free selves, we have nothing of real value to give to others. We are truly impoverished.

The prevailing misunderstanding of the ego self is that we are independent from everything else. This leads to the sense of our selves as the principal actor and the central figure in our life stories, our life dramas. Believing in the reality of this false self leads eventually to all the problems we associate with taking ourselves too seriously. This is how we create our own prisons. Can we let go of the illusion of "me"? Can we let go of our identification with this false self as our real self? If so, only then can we experience the free self. Then we exchange what is less important for what is more important and there is no loss of anything significant. The free self is not only free of society but also of the ego. It does not operate under the illusion of separateness. We are free to become a part of everything. Concerns about what is best for the individual gradually dissolve into concern for the greater good.

When we let go of our identification with the false self, it becomes more difficult to focus on the details of the every-day world—especially in the cases where the everyday world seems preoccupied with things that now seem irrelevant. Out of respect for the feelings of others it may be necessary to act with some semblance of conformity, like a guest in another culture who tries to adhere to proper etiquette. The driving motivations, however, will be connectedness and humility—not indifference or a sense of superiority. If we are too submissive or obedient to outside authority, then we will be giving our freedom to some-one else. If we are too hostile toward the world around us, we will end up attacking the sources of our own happiness, driving away loving connections. To understand the free self is to know how to actively belong in the world without being a prisoner of it. We can be content with the fact that our freedom is finite but not hold back from participating in life responsibly, meaning-fully, and uniquely.

We are like swimmers in the middle of an enormous river trying to stay afloat while being carried along by the strong current. We can spend our time and energy struggling against the flow, or frantically trying to reach the safety of the shore, or we can instead open ourselves up to becoming better swimmers and set our sights downstream. When we try to swim against the cur-rent, we find that it only becomes stronger and gives us greater resistance. But as we learn to swim with it, our swimming grows stronger. If we advance our understanding of the current and learn how to cooperate with it, we will increase our ability to decide where we would like to go and we can even use it to help us get there. The power of the river's flow will then become a source of our own ever-growing power. And the use of this power will be less a matter of taking a steady and predictable direction and more about improving our agility, flexibility and adaptability for coping with widely divergent circumstances.

We do not need to wage a battle with the outside world to become free. Freedom is our higher nature. No one else can give it to us. We can only liberate ourselves. And we can only do it directly. It does not require anyone else's permission. Although we can learn a great deal from the crowd, we should never let the opinions of others become our boundaries. We should never let the crowd tell us what is right. That could only lead us to be obedient or defiant, but never free.

When we are young, our consciences are shaped by our parents, teachers, friends, religion, and culture; the process of becoming oneself requires us to grow through these influences, to assimilate and eventually transcend them to the point where our inner intelligence decides what is right. Our inner intelligence can make use of all the wisdom that is available from the crowd while at the same time finding its own way by its own means. The moment we are unafraid of the crowd, we become free to be ourselves, and life immediately begins to take on a new and better quality. No one can ever reach greatness without the freedom to give his or her own intelligence the ultimate authority. Conformity puts us in chains; freedom gives us wings.

CHAPTER TWENTY–SEVEN
Spiritual Awareness

"All day long I think about it, then at night I say it. Where did I come from and what am I supposed to be doing? I have no idea. My soul is from elsewhere, I'm sure of that, and I intend to end up there."– Jalal al-Din Rumi

Conventional awareness, with its strong orientation toward individuality and materialism, leaves many of us with an uncomfortable feeling of disconnectedness. In fact, the more we think of "I" as something discrete and independent, the more we intensify our feeling of separation from the world around us, making us vulnerable to issues of insecurity and loneliness. By contrast, spiritual awareness is the conscious concern for the inner life of mind and spirit, and our relationship with all that exists beyond the visible world. Spiritual awareness stimulates our powers of observation and insight, rendering us more able to comprehend a reality with many layers and textures.

As we achieve greater levels of spiritual awareness, our perspective naturally evolves from one of intense self-absorption toward a realm of global wholeness. There occurs a weakening of the tension between "I" and "other" as we come to understand our inseparable connectedness with everything else. This happens not by the diminishment of individual self, but rather from the expansion of our concept of self to include so much more than "me" and "mine." In this expanded understanding, nothing of value about our individuality need be sacrificed, just the illusion that "I" exist separately from everything else.

This level of awareness can only be experienced through intuitive powers. It is a knowing beyond logical reasoning because logical reasoning derives its truth from the physical senses, which perceive "things" whereas intuition perceives processes. The deeply intuitive person has learned to think and understand through the use of relatively flexible conceptual structures. Such individuals can tune into higher frequencies of consciousness, shifting from mechanical realities to fluid realities. In effect, higher consciousness uses logical thinking as a ladder that is climbed to a certain height for the purpose of jumping off and taking flight. Once we feel the power of our wings, we will have less need for the ladder. The breadth of understanding that is subsequently realized through intuitive flight can no longer be supported by the ladder of logic—but it doesn't have to be. At the level of spiritual awareness, we don't allow the ladder to hold us back. We can distinguish between the benefits of common logic and the limitations we impose on our intelligence when we confuse logic with wisdom.

As spiritual awareness expresses itself through our inner intelligence, we begin to recognize the interrelatedness of a highly differentiated world. We find ourselves starting to disconnect from our conventional views of life, which then allows us to begin re-connecting again in a new and better way. We realize that we have only relative existence, not independent existence, but more importantly we know that we still belong to it all. This level of realization may seem counter-intuitive to many, but it is actually "purely intuitive." It is only counter-logical.

Unlike religion, spiritual awareness does not have a tendency to become competitive. If we are advancing spiritually, it will not be very important that people agree with us because we will have less need to look to others for validation or acceptance. This is not to say that we will become indifferent to the rest of the world. We may want to explain ourselves to others as clearly as possible in order to help them understand us or to facilitate their own spiritual awareness, but if they are not receptive there should be no sense of rejection and no need for negative feelings. Keeping in mind the fact that we are all flawed and limited should help us to avoid labeling others as "bad," "selfish," or "wrong." Whereas religion can divide people into conflicting groups when it is too focused on secular power, the principles of deep spirituality will have uniting effects. Generally, the ideas that concern spiritual awareness are love, peace, forgiveness, kindness, and gratitude.

Spiritual awareness does not require one to abandon the attractions of everyday life. It is more a matter of re-contextualizing, restructuring and re-envisioning our relationship with everyday life. It brings about a deep personal commitment, but this commitment is focused more on the methodology of exploration and not on a specific set of beliefs. The major focus is not so concerned about a destination, but rather an orientation to our journey. Spiritual awareness is not the same as spiritual ambition. It is not aggressive, competitive, or egotistical. The point of spiritual awareness is not to achieve salvation but to transcend the illusion of separateness, to be free of the world of "me" and "mine" which is the source of so much preventable suffering and unhappiness.

Those with deep spiritual awareness are often socially humble people. They find ways to serve the world simply by what they become. What they know about life they carry calmly within themselves, and this knowledge is not based on faith but on the depth of their own experience. It is their personal understanding of reality and they trust it by virtue of its intrinsic merit and the adaptive power it brings to them. If asked, they can explain it, but without the need to convince others of its final and absolute truth because they themselves are improving on it continuously.

CHAPTER TWENTY-EIGHT

Love

"Love is the only sane and satisfactory answer to the problem of human existence." — **Erich Fromm**

Love is not merely an emotion; it is the highest level of consciousness. It is an inclusive, expansive, compassionate way of relating to the world. Of all the states of consciousness, love achieves the purest synchronicity with the conditions of our existence because it rises above all of life's contentious dichotomies and easily transcends negativity. Where greed only wants and never gives, love, in its purest form, is an unconditional sharing that never asks for anything in return. From an emotional standpoint, nothing can be needed beyond love.

Love is not something we acquire but a potential born within us. It comes with being human. To be developed it must be experienced, and must be experienced in order to be understood. The laws of love cannot be scripted by society. They are encoded in the heart where moral laws and commandments have no jurisdiction. Our heart knows what each of us deeply needs to become ourselves. The human growth process requires lots of love, not in the form of neediness but rather the kind of love that is a sharing. When this higher form of love is activated, our individuality is not sacrificed but expanded in its form because we are drawing power from the highest energy field we can ever experience. The more we love, the more we increase our capability to love.

Much of popular culture presents love as something we get, an experience that has to be deserved, and that is part of an exchange. In this model, the more we give away without receiving any in return, the less we will have. But the very opposite is the truth. If we are looking to another to give us love, then we are already without it; we are already living in a state of lacking. When we believe that the love we need is in the other person and when the other person believes that the love they need is in us, we will both eventually feel cheated. The love we are looking for will not arrive from someone else if we do not know how to cultivate it first in ourselves. There is no other way to be receptive to mature love.

Two people who start out empty and alone as individuals will only be capable of creating a relationship in which they end up empty and alone together. On the other hand, when two loving people share their love with each other, they take part in an almost paradoxical process by which the special synergy of their interconnection brings them more closely and intimately together, even as it expands their sense of freedom and enhances their individual development. People need close and lasting attachments to particular others. In order for our lives to have meaning, we need to give and take and share. We are full of emotions that seek to be finely tuned for expressing love.

The logical mind has its limitations. It does not have the capacity to know love. Love is not logical. It can be felt and experienced in many ways, but never fully comprehended. Even when we are deeply in love, can we say that we understand love? Can we ever reduce the experience to knowledge? Only the heart can comprehend love, and the heart does not operate primarily through the intellect but through the emotions. Feeling is a different form of knowing. The poets and artists are much more effective at understanding and expressing this realm of human experience. The intuitive mind, however, is designed to help us mature and evolve in expressions of love. Those who are deeply open to love have invested the greater part of their trust and energy in enhancing their ability to *feel* love's effects.

Love is our deepest need, but it is also our greatest risk. There is perhaps no emotional challenge more daunting to our sense of security, yet nothing leads a person along his or her path of growth more than love. It is much easier to contemplate love than to open up to it. The ideal love is easy to imagine, however love in real life is not a state of Nirvana. No one has ever loved another without problems. Love as a relationship is in fact a lower level of love. It is filled with hazards because it highlights our deepest vulnerabilities. Love relationships require us to grow, and growing is never easy and often painful. That is why being in love will always keep us on the edge of our comfort zones. Love is the greatest growth imperative of all, but it requires an inner growth. It does not help when we project our demands, expectations, and frustrations onto the other person.

We seek love because it is the most cherished human experience. It is the best use we can make of life, the best reward we can take from life, and the best asset we can ever offer. With love we rise above the mundaneness of everyday existence. Without it we may not be particularly unhappy, and we will almost certainly have fewer troubles to deal with—but people who are loveless are essentially lifeless. A person may claim to be healthy because he or she doesn't have any major diseases, but the mere absence of illness does not, in itself, define physical or emotional vitality.

Imagine if the primary aim of life was to avoid those situations in which major problems might arise. This would require that we protect ourselves against the very vulnerabilities that love exposes us to. We would look for ways to be undisturbed and undistracted, but we could not tolerate the discomfort of discovering deep abiding happiness. We would value stillness above joy, fulfillment, and celebration. A life of pure contentment may be quiet and untroubled, but such a life has little intrinsic worth. If we are to learn how to love another, the most important lessons must always be learned first within ourselves. This is dangerous work but if we are courageous and persistent we will succeed. Each of us is the basic unit of the love that is ubiquitous in Nature. We are descendents of love. That is why love is the most significant, most essential element in our being.

CHAPTER TWENTY–NINE
Compassion

*"How far you go in life depends on your being tender with
the young, compassionate with the aged, sympathetic with
the striving and tolerant of the weak and strong...
because someday in life you will have been all of these."*
— **George Washington Carver**

Compassion is one of our greatest sources of emotional power, and the highest expression of love.
It is not a distinctive emotional energy, but rather a state of awareness that refines and transforms all of our other life energies. It
does not emerge from passion or desire, as love does. In fact,
we seem to grow more familiar with our potential for compassion when our other desires become less insistent. Compassion
cannot be developed through discipline or obedience because
it is not acquired, but already within us. It doesn't come from
the effort to care. The energy of compassion is liberated by our

deeper understanding of interconnectedness and interdependence. That is why we do not need to learn how to be compassionate, though we do need to learn how not to block it.

If we look around us for the finest examples of human happiness, we see that they are usually brought about by those who wish for the happiness of others. Conversely, when we examine the world's preventable miseries, we see that they are generally caused by those who wish first for their own happiness. This is not to say that self-interest is the natural enemy of compassion. If we deeply understand the interdependent nature of our own existence, then we are able to see more of ourselves in others. We realize that the higher self is fundamentally inclusive and unselfish. In fact, helping others becomes a self-fulfilling effort because it is a mere extension of self-caring. It is a joy, not a sacrifice.

The purer form of compassion is not about having pity for the less fortunate, which only encourages a sense of superiority. Compassion involves a deeper form of kindness than charity, which is often calculated to meet moral or ethical objectives. If we are kind and helpful toward others mainly for the sake of receiving something in return, then our intention is ultimately self-centered and self-serving. We may be helping others but we are also using others. We should not practice charity for the purpose of gaining the upper hand. True compassion is simply about letting caring and sharing come forth out of our feelings of gratitude and love. A person who puts a lot of effort into helping others, should do so because he or she is in tune with this level of his or her nature and there is no other way for him or her to be.

Compassion is not about giving in to others for the sake of keeping the peace. Compassion must work hand in hand with wisdom to be effective. We can say yes with compassion, but we must also be able to say no. If we believe that no is the wiser thing to say, it can be said in a caring and courageous spirit. Compassion is seldom wise when it is driven by guilt, and if we are feeling very guilty it is a sign that we are not being compassionate enough toward ourselves. Compassion is not self-denial. If we want our compassion to manifest freely we must remember to include ourselves in our kind and caring attitude.

Although truly compassionate actions are not meant to be reciprocal transactions and thus should not be calculated to gain direct benefits, they do tend to have multiplying beneficial effects. Compassion has the power to expand what is generally good and rewarding beyond the focus on a particular set of outcomes. The very display of compassion encourages the best qualities in others. Our greatest happiness comes about from being connected to the well being of others. This is the principle of enlightened self-interest. It recognizes that because we are interdependent, having an attitude of love and kindness toward others is a matter of sound logic. It is the reason why growing toward our potential is our most important responsibility in life and it comes about through the effort of trying to extend the boundaries of self far beyond the world of me, myself and I.

The more our compassion is put into action, the more we will recognize that we are growing in the direction of our own purpose; that is toward our higher self. Nothing of our individual significance is diminished. That which is most important about us as individuals is only heightened when we are motivated to help others. Our energies become more refined and this refinement shows in the quality of every effort we make. In the state of compassion we will not feel like separate islands. Perhaps this is why depression seems to be more prevalent in societies where the emphasis on the individual is greater than the commitment to the common good.

Unbridled individualism will always be self destructive to individuals as well as to groups. If we are motivated to live a life that is worthwhile to ourselves and to others, it means that we are developing our gifts for the sake of giving them. Acting on these feelings will transform situations for the better, no matter what. We simply look to give what is needed when it is needed— assuring that every action is at its core a kind of giving—and we let the rest take care of itself.

CHAPTER THIRTY

Conscious Intention
(Giving Direction and Momentum to Life)

"From intention springs the deed, from the deed springs the habits. From the habits grow the character, from character develops destiny." — **from a Chinese Buddhist text**

Our every action is preceded by an intention, though unfortunately the intention is often unconscious and is brought about through the operation of our habit systems. We may desire to live a positive life, but if our patterns of thought and action are rooted in anger, fear, or depression, our minds will perpetuate repeated patterns of negative behavior. Our lives are mostly subject to what we hold in mind. Whatever we frequently think about or reflect on will become the primary inclination of our conditioned responses. Since energy follows thought, what we think about will have causal effects. What we do now or what we allow to happen next will affect what will happen in the future.

If we are determined to live from the intentions of respect and kindness, we must learn to use our thoughts to shape a more respectful and kind future.

So much of what we think, feel, and do results from automaticity rather than conscious pre-intention, but our habits are not unchangeable. Not only is it possible to choose the way we think, but also to change the way we think. Of course we will feel many different motivations because the mind is enormously complex, but which are the wisest? To which motivations should we attach our intentions? For example, we might establish a habit of saying each morning, "Today is going to be one of the greatest days of my life...because this is the one I'm in." By aligning our conscious awareness with our most important intentions, we can chart the course for both our conscious and unconscious processes.

The most effective way to direct our energies is to clarify our deepest motivations, bring them to conscious awareness, and then act on premeditated intentions. Each time we consciously direct our mental abilities in this way and then follow our conscious intentions, we are establishing or reinforcing our chosen behavioral patterns at the point where they originate. We are planting seeds in our minds that will begin to grow as we come into contact with conditions that support them.

Through even our smallest actions, we are putting causal relationships into motion that will influence the future. And by creating a healthier future we also transform the past. As in the analogy of the two arrows, the first arrow cannot be changed; it has already happened. And yet, it can either be firmly established in our memory as a negative experience or converted instead into positive outcomes. This conversion from the negative to the positive cannot be achieved unless we fully accept the first arrow. Once we do this, the first arrow will help put us back into growth mode.

Every day we are receiving results from the past, and quite often in the form of our own self-limiting thoughts. Through the intelligent use of conscious intention, we can respond in ways that create new and better thought patterns. Without a reflective pause there will only be the automatic reaction, which preserves the dysfunctional relationship between past, present, and future. Particularly during times of strife, it is good to stop and ask ourselves if we are trying to get even, or trying to become happier and wiser.

Making each moment a reflection of our truest intentions, our most important values, and our highest priorities is an extremely compelling way to live. No matter what difficulties we are facing, conscious intention allows us to remain cognizant of where we are and where we wish to go. In the final analysis, the kind of person we become mentally, emotionally and spiritually will be a result primarily of our inner decisions, and not the result of our environment. As we strengthen the habit of watching our mind from the quiet and secure stillness of inner awareness, we enjoy a greater freedom to adapt to life's continuous changes, to protect ourselves and others from the ugliness of negativity, and to create a positive mental state at any point in time.

We should seek to make our overarching intention to become a self that operates with the confidence and control to choose freely, to dictate action, to openly receive both pleasure and pain, and to optimize each situation regardless of the conditions we're given. If we keep our conscious intentions focused on bringing quality, discovering quality, and deriving quality from each and every moment, the cumulative effect will be a quality life. Eventually we become like the eagle at mid-afternoon, who begins to soar not from the flapping of its wings but by gliding with the updrafts. As we learn to become better gliders, the forces of free will and determinism combine synergistically and there is little else for us to do but to become attuned to our deepening intelligence. Life will take us where we need to go.

CHAPTER THIRTY–ONE
Responsibility

"I recommend that the Statue of Liberty on the East Coast be supplemented by a Statue of Responsibility on the West Coast."
—Vicktor Frankl

There is a fundamental interrelationship between responsibility and freedom. If they do not both exist together, then neither one can exist separately. When we refuse to take responsibility for our own lives, we are essentially relinquishing our freedom in other ways. There are many things in life that are beyond our direct control, but the most important controlling function we possess as a human being is the freedom to choose our mental state. When we exercise the power this freedom affords us, all the choices we make and whatever eventuates from those choices is our responsibility.

It is one level of achievement to become free from outside control, but then an even greater issue arises. "What will I do when I am free?" If we fail to take responsibility for the things we are free to control, we will eventually lose control of those things too. That is why responsibility is the prerequisite of freedom. Until we are willing to take full responsibility for our own lives, our actions, thoughts, and consequences, we will not gain the freedom to grow to our fullest selves.

Our most basic psychological needs are to love and be loved, to develop our talents, and to contribute to the greater good in a meaningful way. If we devote ourselves to these, we grow by learning to give the best of ourselves in ways that have powerful meaning. This involves coming to terms with values and purposes that go beyond our day-to-day needs. Through this process we can become more aware of our natural gifts and also realize that our natural gifts always point us toward our responsibilities. If we choose to avoid these responsibilities we undermine our freedom to participate fully in this growth process. Thus, we will be the primary agents of our own underachievement.

We are not really free in an environment where the only correct choice is to obey, nor are we free where we do not have to take responsibility for our choices and their consequences. That is why the greatest discipline is self-discipline. Only those who are self-disciplined can rise above the state of being obedient to others. Self-discipline gives us a strong inner will to do what is not easy; to do the difficult growth-work that our weaker natures will resist doing. But this is the only way to attain the inner freedom to be self-determining.

It is a weakness to always be seeking our shelter in somebody else's rules, but we will need others' rules if we lack the mental strength to be obedient to our own inner intelligence. Once we reach the level of independence where there is no one who can force us to behave a certain way, it is up to us to decide what decisions and behaviors are best. When we come to own these decisions, we will also own their consequences and the consequences will tell us when our decisions are wise and when they are foolish. This is how our freedom is earned, and this is how we will use our freedom if we are being responsible.

Inner freedom in itself does not guarantee our happiness. It is a necessary condition but not sufficient. It merely gives us the opportunity to become responsible. Only by responsibility can we exercise our innate power to create a happy life. And if we remain stuck in a weak and unhappy state of mind, that too is our responsibility. It will be so because we have chosen it.

There are those who truly believe that they are not responsible for their own attitudes, as though one's attitude is not a voluntary thing but an automatic reaction to life's circumstances. Not surprisingly, these are usually the same people who display more negative attitudes. They are free all along to choose happiness, yet they allow others to determine whether their day will be good or bad. As soon as we put this responsibility on someone else, we are exchanging our freedom for frustration.

The feeling of frustration will come because we will have given away the prerogative to experience our lives as we want to experience them. If we choose to put the blame for our frustration on others, we put ourselves at the mercy of others, because we cannot change anybody else. One of the most unfulfilled wishes in the world is to change someone else. The only transformation we can possibly achieve is our own, and it is our responsibility to make that a top priority.

CHAPTER THIRTY–TWO
Accepting Death

*"A fear of death follows from the fear of life. A man who lives
fully is prepared to die at any time."* — **Mark Twain**

We are alive, therefore we will die. This is the simplest, most
obvious learned truth of our existence and yet very few of us
are inclined to honestly come to terms with it. Children do not
initially comprehend death, but by school age have come to see
that life is impermanent. From this age we learn that someday
life will end but as long as we harbor a deep-seated aversion to
openly contemplating death we will never learn to accept it
with our hearts. If we aspire to live consciously, fully, and lov-
ingly, we will want to approach our relationship with death in
the same way. We do not have to think of death as something
heavy, dark, and tragic, but a healthier view would require us to
step away from the concepts of evil and punishment, which have
embedded the fear of death into our minds.

Modern culture has contributed to the avoidance and fear of death as a final reality by conditioning us to be uncomfortable and avoid the whole topic whenever possible. We are encouraged instead to use our time and energy for the pursuit of such things as material possessions, reputation, popularity, and physical pleasures. Furthermore, we use these material, financial, and social distractions to divert our attention from the fear of our ultimate demise and the demise of all the people we know.

Many people are either living in denial of death or in terror of it, as if the thought or reality itself were the natural enemy of happiness. It is not. The natural enemy of happiness is fear. Accepting the true conditions of life, including the finality of death for all, is the only legitimate road to a deep and abiding happiness. When we are in resistance mode we cannot be open and accepting of what is happening; only by being open and accepting of our conditions can we ever have a chance to achieve harmony with them. If we are striving to become our best selves, we must also strive to know ourselves; this includes knowing the reality of our situation. Perhaps the most difficult aspect of our situation for us to know and accept is the interrelatedness of life and death.

Society has divided life and death into distinctly separate realms and created a mutually hostile existence between them. This perspective has been most un-conducive to our well-being. The challenge we are left with is to re-combine the notions of life and death in our understanding just as they are combined in reality. People commonly refer to staying alive as defying death, or they speak of death as robbing us of life, and talk about noble battles with death, which present it as some external enemy. These are merely representations of our ignorance. When we observe Nature, we see that the sprout comes into being only through the disintegration of the seed. We do not say that the seed loses its battle against the sprout, or that the sprout should resist the coming of the blooming plant. The plant does not feel trepidation with each sign of autumn's impending arrival. What good can come from fearing our own Nature, when it is that same Nature that brought forth this precious life we are experiencing?

Keeping the thought of our own death close by at all times will actually serve to make life sweeter. Long have we been told at countless funerals and other solemn events that the more we come to appreciate the reality of life's impermanence the more predisposed our minds will be to recognizing what a wonderful gift today is. But do we carry this wise advice into our day-to-day lives? Our minds are generally more inclined to suppress this information and instead to pursue other distractions to push away this fearful awareness.

When we awake each morning, it would be a good practice to reflect briefly on the fact that this day could be our last. Continual affirmation of this truth will help us place a greater importance on the present moment as well as reinforce our determination to live a full and rich life. If we believe that our life is a truly precious gift, the best way to show it is not simply to cling to it, but to use our time and talents for **the good**. Tomorrow can be a very wasteful concept if we use it to delay giving the best of ourselves today.

Just as the seasons are perpetually changing, we are part of a dynamic process that is always continuing through, transforming from something into something else. When we remember that the conscious life we now enjoy arises out of the changing seasons of birth and death, we can see the inherent futility in wishing for personal happiness but not wanting to accept death as an inevitable part of life. In essence, it is the same as saying that we want to partake enthusiastically in all of the blessings and opportunities this process bestows during the season of life, while at the same time fearing and resisting the thought of going where it is ultimately taking us. Until we are able to come to terms with the reality of our impermanence and openly accept life's limitations, we cannot be fully open to its possibilities.

No one knows for sure what it will be like to die. Death is an enigma, but then so too is life. It is pointless to live in fear of either. However, we show wisdom and maturity by preparing for death throughout life. If our approach to living and dying is balanced and congruent, we can be free to make the most of life while avoiding the extremes of being too morbid or over-indulgent. As our fear of death diminishes, there will be less cause to be preoccupied with unwholesome thoughts or feelings about it; as our sense of gratitude and connectedness expands, the need to escape into self-indulgence will gradually give way to expressions of self-responsibility.

The art of living and the art of dying do not belong to mutually exclusive realms; they are highly interdependent. Living well and dying well are contrasting phases of the same continuum; both call upon the same higher values of love, compassion, courage, gratitude, and happiness. If we learn to spend our days cultivating these qualities, they will be the characteristic strengths that define us, sustain us, and allow us to help our loved ones whenever the ends of our lives come. Simply put, a deeply meaningful life, committed to growth until our last breath, should naturally lead to a deeply meaningful death. And when it is time to transition from this world to whatever is next, if we have lived more fully, we can expect to die happier and more fulfilled people.

CHAPTER THIRTY–THREE
Bringing It All Together

*"All the greatest and most important problems of life are
fundamentally unsolvable… They can never be solved but only
outgrown. This 'outgrowing' proves on further investigation to
require a new level of consciousness… It is not solved logically
in its own terms but fades when confronted with a new and
stronger life force."* — **Carl Jung**

This book has described the beginning steps to becoming oneself. It is intended to whet the appetite by describing the upper
possibilities of being human and suggesting what we can do
to move ourselves along the continuum of our own potential.
There is never a better place to start than within our own minds.
If we are not taking responsibility for our mental states, then we
are not taking responsibility for our lives. What is involved is a
process of slowly removing the underpinnings of our ignorance
and immaturities. The work required is often quite difficult

but whatever progress we make will always be its own reward. The selves that exist beyond these immaturities are powerful, thoughtful, gentle, spontaneous, content, motivated, aware, and generally appreciative of the gift of existence. They are selves well worth liberating.

Going from unconscious tendencies to conscious intentional living is the work of a lifetime, but the essence of self-awakening is that once we begin to truly understand who we are, we cannot stay as we are. We do not remain unmoved or unchanged. It is not even possible to move toward the upper reaches of our potential until we begin to make a real effort to change. In proportion to the intensity and wisdom of this effort, we can enjoy the ability to shift our lives into growth mode at any time and in any situation. Through greater self-understanding we learn to willfully transform the way we conduct our daily routines, giving both our challenges and our opportunities a different quality of attention.

Consciousness itself is not a thing to be contained but a universal energy we tap into. Attempts to rigidly control conscious thought only diminish the human spirit. Higher intelligence has more to do with our ability to cooperate with this energy rather than acquiring and possessing it. The more we come to experience and appreciate the essential mutuality of our relationship with everything else, the less our everyday activities will be motivated by the desire for control, nor will we have much use for fear, worry, jealousy, or other anxieties. That which is inwardly or outwardly negative will become increasingly less attractive, less welcome, and less persuasive as the ease and quality of our lives improve. There will be little need to run away from any aspect of our natures because we will see the uselessness of living in fear of the truth, of our potential, of death, and, most importantly, of each other.

The innate abilities to acquire intelligence throughout life, to adjust our course, imagine future possibilities, strive toward difficult goals, and recover from our setbacks, constitute our strongest qualifications for taking charge of our own growth. If we assertively utilize these abilities, by deciding what *we* want to do with the next moment, and the moment after that, we will rarely be limited to just one chance to move forward. Life may send us ten, a hundred, or a thousand occasions to define ourselves and to shape our situations into what they need to be.

Becoming ourselves is not a function of searching for the most ideal external conditions. It begins with the recognition that our greatest opportunities always originate within the realm of conscious mind. This is where the most important work is done and this is also where the rewards are most deeply experienced. Not all life conditions lead to physical health, to material wealth, to conventional success, or to broad popularity, but all conditions have the potential to lead us toward wisdom, positive meaning, and fulfillment. Beyond that, how can we feel that the world owes us anything?

Confronting reality in all its forms as a potentiality to be explored and tested is not an activity for the weak of heart. We are more likely to commit to this search when we trust there is something profoundly important to find, something with a deeper meaning for our lives. Imbedded in this commitment is the personal conviction that we belong to a Universe in which our existence has significance. As we continue to grow in our awareness of what that significance is, we find ourselves becoming more consciously and functionally harmonious with everything around us. Our thought processes and activities accommodate a more finely balanced interplay between taking charge and letting go, between embracing what is unavoidable and knowing how and when to assert the creative power of free will.

It is both possible and rational to accept the inevitable realities of our world while remaining highly motivated to change the world; to take it all in while purposefully taking hold of *our* part of it. In so doing, we expand our ability to recognize and cooperate with the circumstances unfolding before us even as we endeavor to keep searching and reaching for what we can make from them. This is the modus operandi of a consciousness that is highly aware of the various patterns of life and how these patterns can generate utilizable momentum and synergy

At this level of awareness, we will continuously evolve because we can, because we want to, and ultimately because we must. The motivation to keep striving and improving is experienced as an internal imperative. Each new level of understanding stimulates a further refinement of the ways we condition our minds through our everyday habits, and it becomes easier to recognize how each moment of each day offers tremendous possibilities for growth. Negativity in general becomes harder to rationalize, and we become more open and receptive to love, beauty, compassion, forgiveness, inspiration, loyalty, gratitude, hope and happiness—in other words, all that constitutes the actual core and reality of the best human meaning and most beneficial desires. Thus intelligent energy flows more freely and we grow ever more accomplished at the art of becoming ourselves.

Epigraphy

Carl Jung (1875 – 1961) - Swiss psychiatrist often considered the first modern psychologist to state that the human psyche is "by nature religious" and to explore it in depth.

Lao-tzu (appr. 600 - 300 BC) – Chinese Taoist philosopher who encouraged his followers to observe and seek to understand the laws of nature; to develop intuition and build up personal power; and to use that power to lead life with love, and without force.

Henry David Thoreau (1817 – 1862) – American author, poet, philosopher and leading Transcendentalist. He is best known for his book *Walden*, a reflection on simple living in natural surroundings. His philosophy of civil disobedience influenced the political thinking of such later figures as Leo Tolstoy, Mahatma Gandhi, and Martin Luther King, Jr.

Saul Bellow (1915 – 2005) – Jewish-American novelist and recipient of both the Pulitzer Prize and the Nobel Prize for Literature. He was known for his penetrating insights about modern life in America after World War II.

Johann Wolfgang von Goethe (1749 – 1832) – German writer and philosopher considered by many to be the most important writer in the German language and one of the most important thinkers in Western culture.

Norman Vincent Peale (1898 – 1993) – American minister and author, most notably of *The Power of Positive Thinking*. His radio show *The Art of Living* ran for 54 years and was extremely popular during the Great Depression.

Ralph Waldo Emerson (1803 – 1882) – American lecturer, essayist, and poet who led the New England Transcendentalist movement. He was a champion of individualism and a critic of the conforming pressures of society.

Will Rogers (1879 - 1935) – American cowboy, humorist, actor, social commentator, columnist, radio personality, and one of the most popular American celebrities of the 1920s and 30s.

Osho (1931 – 1990) – Indian mystic, radical philosopher, and spiritual teacher who garnered an international following.

Shantideva (8ᵗʰ Century) – Indian Buddhist scholar at Nalanda University. He was the author of "A Guide to the Bodhisattva's Way of Life," a long poem describing the process of enlightenment from the first thought to full Buddhahood.

Salman Rushdie (1947) – British-Indian novelist and essayist whose style is often classified as magical realism mixed with historical fiction. A dominant theme of his works is the story of the many connections and disruptions between the Eastern and Western worlds.

Albert Camus (1913 – 1960) French Algerian author, philosopher, and journalist whose views contributed to the rise of the philosophy known as *absurdism*. His most famous novel was *The Stranger*. He was awarded the Nobel Prize for Literature.

Emile Durkheim (1858 – 1917) – French social scientist who formerly established sociology as an academic discipline along with Karl Marx and Max Weber. His insights came from studying phenomena attributed to society at large rather than the specific acts of individuals.

Mother Teresa (1910 – 1997) – Catholic nun and humanitarian of Albanian ethnicity and Indian citizenship who ministered to the poor, sick, orphaned, and dying. She was awarded the Nobel Peace Prize.

Khalil Gibran (1887 – 1931) – Lebanese American artist, poet, and writer. He is chiefly known for his 1923 book *The Prophet*, a series of inspirational philosophical essays.

Abraham Maslow (1908 - 1970) – Psychologist who became the leader of the humanistic school of psychology, which was based on the premise that every person has a strong desire to realize his or her full potential. He is best known for his Hierarchy of Needs.

Lin Yutang (1895 – 1976) – Chinese writer and inventor whose compilations and translations of classic Chinese texts into English were bestsellers in the West. He was one of the most influential writers of his generation.

Madeleine L'Engle (1918 – 2007) – American writer best known for her Young Adult fiction. Her works reflected both her Christian faith and her strong interest in modern science.

Confucius (551 – 479 BC) – Chinese logician and social philosopher who emphasized personal and governmental morality, correctness of social relationships, justice, and sincerity. His thoughts have been developed into a system of philosophy known as *Confucianism*.

Vaclav Havel (1936) – Czech playwright, essayist, dissident, and politician whose human rights activism led to his imprisonment. He was a central figure in the "Velvet Revolution," which brought radical political change in his nation. He was the last President of Czechoslovakia and the first President of the Czech Republic.

Thomas Merton (1915 – 1968) – American Catholic writer, Trappist monk, and student of comparative religion who wrote on spirituality, social justice, and a quiet pacifism. He was a proponent of interfaith understanding who pioneered dialogue with prominent Asian spiritual figures including the Dalai Lama, D.T. Suzuki, and Thich Nhat Hanh.

Macus Tillius Cicero (106 BC – 43 BC) – Roman politician, lawyer, orator, and philosopher, he is widely considered one of Rome's greatest orators. His speeches and letters remain some of the most important primary sources of the last days of the Roman Republic.

Guatama Buddha (563 BC– 483 BC) – Spiritual leader from ancient India and founder of Buddhism. He is said to have realized complete insight into the causes of suffering and the steps necessary to eliminate it. These discoveries became known as the "Four Noble Truths," which are the heart of Buddhist teaching.

George Herbert (1593 – 1633) – Welsh poet, orator, and Anglican priest. Throughout his life he wrote religious poems and hymns. He was described by one literary historian as "a soul composed of harmonies."

Paulo Coelho (1947) – Brazilian lyricist and novelist, he authored the novel *The Alchemist* in 1987 about a poor Spanish shepherd boy who journeyed across Africa in search of treasure and learned to turn all of his obstacles into blessings by following his heart.

Jalal al-Din Rumi (1207 – 1273) – Persian mystical poet of Islam. His works have been widely translated into many of the world's languages and their importance has transcended national and ethnic boundaries.

Erich Fromm (1900 – 1980) – German social psychologist, psychoanalyst, and humanistic philosopher. He was associated with what became known as the Frankfort School of Critical Theory. He believed that freedom was an aspect of human nature that we either embrace or escape.

George Washington Carver (1864 – 1943) – African American born into slavery who became a scientist, botanist, educator, and inventor. He led the Agricultural Department at Tuskegee University for 47 years, teaching former slaves farming techniques for self-sufficiency.

Vicktor Frankl (1905 – 1997) – Austrian neurologist and psychiatrist as well as a Holocaust survivor. He was the founder of logotherapy, which is a form of existential analysis. His best-known book, *Man's Search for Meaning,* chronicles his experiences as a concentration camp inmate and describes his psychotherapeutic method of finding meaning in all forms of existence.

Mark Twain (1835 – 1910) – American author, lecturer, and humorist who is best known for his novels *The Adventures of Tom Sawyer* and *Adventures of Huckleberry Finn* (often cited as *the* "Great American Novel"). Twain was a friend to presidents, artists, industrialists, and European royalty.

EBOOK AND KINDLE
EDITIONS
ALSO AVAILABLE

WA